Enjoy
Your
Healing Power

Copyright © *Katia de Peyer,* 2025

All Rights Reserved

ISBN (paperback): 979-8-9915655-1-6
ISBN (ebook): 979-8-9915655-0-9

Published by La Source Press

This book is subject to the condition that no part of this book is to be reproduced, transmitted in any form or means; electronic or mechanical, stored in a retrieval system, photocopied, recorded, scanned, or otherwise. Any of these actions require the proper written permission of the author.

Enjoy Your Healing Power

KATIA DE PEYER

To my grandchildren Loren, Anna and Devon

ACKNOWLEDGMENTS

Enjoy Your Healing Power is a work of love. It could not have emerged without the superb review and edit of Valerie Aubry. With infinite patience, clarity and a deep understanding of the subject, Valerie has given her all to this work. Her long experience as an editor at Oxford University Press and elsewhere is of immense value to anyone who works with her, as I did, as a guide, advisor and editor.

Wayne Ensrud, a superb artist and dear friend of many years, offered his wit and whimsical spirit in this text's images. An immensely gifted painter, Wayne graced the text with his own poetic vision.

I want to thank all who have supported this work, among others my friend Janet Hubbard, the well-known author of *Vengeance in the Vineyard Mysteries* and *The Eloquence of Grief* whose thoughtful encouragement in reading the manuscript was invaluable. Emily Fritz offered helpful editorial and design support in preparing the manuscript for publication.

Finally, my gratitude goes to Reiki Master Ethel Lombardi whose inspiration in tuning her students to the Mari-El energy offered a whole new field of spiritual investigation.

Contents

Acknowledgments — 7

Introduction — 1

1 Healing Is Part of Our Heritage — 11

2 Know Thyself — 49

3 Our Spiritual Anatomy — 77

4 Healing — 105

5 Hands-On Healing — 119

6 Dancing With Life — 135

Epilogue — 149

INTRODUCTION

Enjoy your Healing Power is a guide to awaken the dormant power within us, to heal ourselves, our fellow living beings and our world. Our goal is to activate this innate power. We will share common insights, concepts and practices that have guided healers through the ages, and use this work's design like a map. We will survey the terrain first and then practice as it guides us home to our healing power.

What is Healing?

Healing is nature's way of restoring balance and harmony in our being. It transforms a state of inner repression or conflict to one of clarity and ease, one in which our physical, emotional, mental, and spiritual faculties are in sync.

So much of what happens in the outer world, including all the information that bombards us, overwhelms the finer senses that make us aware of how we really feel. Since our physical state expresses our inner state, it is vital that we become conscious of the sensations that lie deep within our body's memory. Our body has its own intelligence that yearns to be understood. Our health depends on our ability to learn our body's language and make wise use of the self-knowledge it provides.

The key that unlocks the mystery of our physiology lies in the functioning of our immune system. Natural healing therapies offer a non-invasive way to boost the immune system. Osteopaths, massage therapists, chiropractors, movement therapists and healing practitioners use touch and movements to stimulate the blood and neural and endocrine flow. Their work shows that the immune system is affected by what has been called the human energy field.

I first became aware of energy fields at the conference "Healing in our Times" in Washington DC in 1981 under the auspices of the Sufi Order of NY, chaired by Dr. Elizabeth Kübler-Ross. Distinguished international scientists shared the symposium's panel with mystics and healers of the day. After hearing the healer Ethel Lombardi mentioned, I seized the chance to join her study group on Reiki healing in New York City. One of two healers chosen for study by the National Institutes of Health, Ethel was the last Reiki Master to be initiated by Hawayo Takata whose husband Chujiro Hayashi was the first Master to receive his attunement and degree from Mikao Usui, the man who rediscovered Reiki energy as an ancient key to universal healing in the late eighteen hundred.

As a Reiki Master, Ethel presented her students with signs of her extraordinary mastery of energy fields. At the end of our Reiki I training, she asked us to stand at one end of the room while she sat facing us at the other end. It was early summer and, although late in the day and with her back against daylight, we could see her face clearly. We knew that she was preparing us for a special experience, but not what to expect. She told us that we had to watch her face intently and speak up about what we saw since none of us would see the same thing.

Within seconds, her face lost all definition. Around the edge, a bright light or aura started at first as a dim sight, soon to grow into a bright light two inches wide. Barely adjusting to the extraordinary sight of an aura of this magnitude, I became overwhelmed by what followed. After all these years, I am still speechless at what I witnessed which, even in my dreams, I would never have thought possible. A series of faces, most looking like ancient buddhas, which Ethel later called her guides, started to appear over Ethel's face. Each vision lasted a few seconds, and the whole event lasted for over twenty minutes without interruption. I saw a procession of ancient Asian faces-wise, radiant, severe-all of them of utmost dignity. Among them, I saw the face of what I would later recognize as Ganesha, the gentle Hindu elephant God of the homestead, and the radiant face of an exquisitely beautiful woman whose smile went right to my heart.

With this display, Ethel Lombardi sought to leave an indelible mark in our consciousness so that we would firmly believe in the power of the spirit and our responsibility to make the right use of it. She revealed to us that a new energy which she called Mari-El (Mari for Mary and El for Elohim), was coming to the earth to harmonize the masculine and feminine vibrations of the planet. We needed to anchor this new energy in our hearts. During the many years, I studied with her, Ethel Lombardi would reveal to us what she now called "Freedom energy". We are responsible beings of Light.

I came to realize that faith in our ability to change is the foundation of our healing power. Healing is often referred to as spiritual or faith healing for this reason. But becoming a healer does not require great leaps of faith. Our growing self-awareness nurtures our new belief system over time.

Unless we are mindful of our inner state, our consciousness becomes fragmented and we lose the resilience we need to maintain our equilibrium. As we become aware of a deeper self, we become attuned to the life-giving energy of the universe. Our revitalized being provides life-enhancing sensors that help us experience the divine energy that is all around us. We need to approach life in a new way and let go of old habits of processing information.

Introduction

How do we build a new belief system? With mental discipline and the regular practice of meditation and visualization, we gradually build a sense of wonder and gratitude for the regenerative process of life. The recipe for wholeness is to examine in a new way what we have neglected in the past. Our ability to generate inner stillness brings to consciousness elements of our nature that got separated from the whole. We become aware of suppressed emotions that block the flow of our life energy. The moment unconscious material is made conscious, a healing takes place. A new vista comes to life in our internal landscape. Embarking on a course that brings healing into our lives is like starting a treasure hunt. With anticipation, we begin our journey on the way to uniting body, mind, and spirit.

For centuries, Western culture conditioned us to see our body and soul as separate. When we discover that body and soul are manifestations of the same cosmic energy, we experience our wholeness and oneness with the Universe! From this new perspective comes our ability to heal. We learn to let go of fear and reflect on the spirit of love that is our heritage. The power of our heart gives life to our new beliefs while the warmth of our hands communicates this truth. This is our homecoming, back to the source where we are one with the spirit that animates our healing potential.

The Science of Healing

Today, there is mounting interest in the field of healing. A growing number of medical practitioners and researchers recognize that alternative healing therapies can complement traditional medical practice in valuable ways. The National Institutes of Health, the embodiment of the medical establishment, has formed the Office of Alternate Medicine to evaluate various natural therapies. Major insurance companies reimburse policyholders for some alternative therapies and offer wellness plans. Most medical schools, including Harvard, Yale and Johns Hopkins, now offer courses in alternative medicine.

These changing attitudes are spurred in part by the public's surging interest in alternative healing methods. Over half of Americans have tried such therapies to improve their health often alongside traditional medical treatments. People see such methods as a way to assume greater responsibility for their health and boost their recovery from various illnesses. [1]

Changing attitudes reflect a growing awareness that, while the science of medicine and surgery continues to make great strides, it has its own limitations. These stem from traditional medicine's almost exclusive reliance on a "scientific model" for studying and curing illness that reflects the worldview of the Industrial Revolution that gave rise to it. This model empha-

---

[1] Americans Health Care Behaviors and Use of Conventional and Alternative Medicine. Cary Funk, Brian Kennedy, and Meg Hefferon. Pew Research Center Study. February 2, 2017 https://www.pewresearch.org/science/2017/02/02/americans-health-care-behaviors-and-use-of-conventional-and-alternative-medicine/

sizes drugs and technology over the simple care giving of the past. Successful as it is, it intimates that the body functions as a machine whose parts can be replaced at will, leaving aside the more mysterious aspect of our physiology.

There is a growing recognition that our organism has its own intelligence. Our nervous system's regulation of myriad variables relies on our unconscious faculties as well as on our objective capacity for thinking and planning. Scientific experiments demonstrate that our conscious mind communicates with our unconscious system on an ongoing basis. It is now an accepted medical fact that our physiology is influenced by a constant interaction between mind and body. The cornerstone of the healer's art is a profound understanding of how to influence this body-mind relationship to help us achieve our deepest human potential.

Evidence of the mind's influence over the body through prayers, affirmations, imagery, and visualization techniques has been confirmed by many testimonials:

> A study by Dr. Carl Simonton and Dr Stephanie Matthews found that out of a hundred terminally-ill patients who used imaging techniques, 19% got rid of their cancer completely and 20% had their disease regress. On average, patients doubled their predicted survival time[2].

---
[2] *Getting Well Again*. O. Carl Simonton, MD. Stephanie Matthews-Simonton. Bantam Books, 1980

> A Stanford University study found that women with breast cancer who participated in support groups lived an average of 18 months or longer than those who didn't.
>
> A study by cardiologist Dean Ornish found that a program of meditation, exercise, group support and a low-fat diet can not only halt the progression of heart disease but actually reverse it.

Many dramatic healings of the sick have been attributed to prayers and faith. In Christian cultures, belief in Mary the mother of God has been often accompanied by blessings, ecstasies, and healings. In Lourdes, France, where every year the pilgrimage to Mary attracts thousands of people from all over the world, 75 cases of miraculous healings have been studied since 1947. Among these, 27 cases have been pronounced scientifically inexplicable by a panel of medical doctors[3].

Books surveying the field of healing tend to promote an intellectual understanding of it. *Enjoy your Healing Power* begins where they leave off by helping us put these ideas into practice. For where the journey to healing is concerned, intellectual understanding is only a starting point. To become healers, we must integrate our physical, emotional, mental and spiritual natures. Since our modern world cultivates our mental skills at the expense of others, we must learn to integrate our facul-

---

[3] *Meetings with Mary, Visions of The Blessed Mother.* Janice T. Connell. Ballantine Books, 1995.

ties anew. To do so, we need firsthand experiences that make concerted use of our physical, emotional, mental and spiritual faculties.

To help you experience this integration, *Enjoy your Healing Power* offers guided practices in meditation and visualization as well as a step-by-step description of how to provide a hands-on-healing session. The key insight shared by all healers through the ages is that the universe, "the macrocosm," and human beings, "the microcosm," are governed by the same cosmic laws. These guided activities draw on these principles to nurture your healing power.

Part One surveys cosmic laws and universal principles that have guided healers from ancient times to the present. We review historic sources, including ancient oral knowledge transmitted through the ages and mystery schools as centers of learning. We reflect on the concept of unity that underlies multiplicity and how it helps us understand who and what we are. We explore the symbolic power of numbers and healing insights behind varied representations of Gods in ancient faiths.

Part Two illustrates how these spiritual insights can heal the self. The journey starts with self-knowledge. Reflecting on the relationship of microcosm to macrocosm yields wisdom. We are the Master Builders of our own temple. The practice of mental scanning develops our inner awareness and links our body and mind. To build our temple, to create our "body of light," we examine the Universal Laws which are grounded in the heart center. Through the law of Love, Life is made manifest.

Part Three focuses on our spiritual and physical anatomy and the power of the mind. It differentiates between the brain as our mental equipment and the mind as our thinking function. We examine the relationship between emotions, our endocrine system, and our vital organs. We learn the mental practice of clearing the cellular memory of each organ with specific visualizations and prayers.

Part Four provides step-by-step instructions for conducting a complete healing session with oneself or another person. It reaffirms the concept that Healing is a manifestation of a radical change of attitude: the Mind is power energy, our energy field is sensitive to mental energy and prayers are the highest form of power energy.

Part Five discusses our connection to the universal field of divine energy. We have our own life story woven into the story of our planet. Our ultimate goal is to bring into the third millennium our new consciousness as healers of our planet.

Enjoy your Healing Power guides the reader through practices that cultivate sensory and emotional awareness at their most subtle level. Intuitive faculties, once developed, allow full participation in one's healing process.

CHAPTER ONE

HEALING IS PART OF OUR HERITAGE

My interest in the field of "healing" was awakened many years ago when, as a young teenager, I experienced the benefit of "hands on healing" on my family and myself. I was raised in a family with close ties to the medical establishment. My mother's great uncle Professor Bernay was one of the medical luminaries in his native town of Lyon, France. Shortly after World War Two, my father died in a tragic accident. The traumatic event was taking its toll on everyone in our family. In her grief, my mother turned to an unlikely source by inviting a practitioner called a "radiesthesist" to help us with our varied ailments. I complained of abdominal cramps. The magical hands took the pain away. I was eleven years old and never forgot the gentle healing and timely care.

Later, while in my twenties, my older sister was the victim of a car accident that almost cost her life. For many months, she was in intensive care in a major hospital in Paris. For days, a pulmonary infection prevented her primary surgeon from proceeding with the needed surgery. Although she was in the care of the best team, everything was stalled as the strongest antibiotics had no effect on her case. Time was of the essence. In desperation, I called a friend with a well-deserved reputation as an amateur healer. I had nothing to lose in trying and had complete faith in him, although he needed convincing to dare to come to a hospital! While I waited outside the door for fear of disturbing him, he proceeded with his hands-on-healing on my sister. That night, my sister's fever came down dramatically. The surgery was set for the next day. From that time on, I knew that there was a power within each one of us waiting to be discovered. How can one be worthy of it and cultivate it in all its integrity? As far as I can remember I was looking for an answer.

My first passion as a child was for the inner beauty in movement. After ten years of training, I became a professional ballet dancer and subsequently a Spanish and flamenco dancer. Later on, I came upon the nascent field of movement-awareness and my meeting with Charlotte Selver, one of its pioneers, would prove a Godsend. Charlotte's work on what she called "Sensory Awareness"[4] is nonverbal and offers a fine tuning into the nature of sensing and perception. At last, I had found a mentor

---

[4] *Essential Reiki. A Complete Guide to An Ancient Healing Art.* Diane Stein. The Crossing Press Inc., 1995.

whose work I totally respected for its integrity. Over the years, I became a successful movement therapist and personal trainer, adding practical experience to my own inner development and search. These formative years gave me deep insights into how our minds and bodies relate and how our creativity can inspire us to make fundamental changes in ourselves and lives. I shared such insights in my first book, *Dancing with MySelf*.[5]

In 1981, I began studying Reiki healing with Ethel Lombardi. The word Reiki comes from Sanskrit and means Universal Love Energy. Mikao Usui who rediscovered Reiki healing[6] in the mid-1800's, was a Christian Minister as well as principal of Doshisha University in Kyoto, Japan. Mikao Usui's ten-year quest to rediscover the spiritual healing method of Jesus led him to the Path of Enlightenment, a sudden visionary experience that provided him with spiritual guidance. Mikao Usui found the answers he needed in ancient Sanskrit texts buried in a Zen Buddhist monastery. His Reiki method of hands-on and absent healing requires an attunement to purify the heart and combines meditation and visualization on traditional symbols. The goal is not only to provide worldly healing but to offer enlightenment.

Ethel Lombardi, my teacher, pursued her own quest. Through her spiritual development, she became attuned to new healing energies she called Mari-El and Freedom energy. She became

---

[5] *Dancing with MySelf. Sensuous Exercises for Body, Mind and Spirit*. Katia de Peyer. Nucleus Publications, 1991, revised 2025.

[6] *Essential Reiki*. Diane Stein. The Crossing Press Inc., Freedom, CA 1995.

conscious of the need to harmonize feminine and masculine energies to save the planet. My encounter with her was another key in my development. It inspired the healer within me and led to spiritual renewal. Since then, I have been a full-time healing practitioner and movement therapist. In writing this book, I want to share the understanding and practice it took to develop my healing skills. For me it was a long search, although it doesn't have to be. I believe that together with making spiritual practice a way of life, understanding our evolution is fundamental to our development as healers.

But first…

What is Healing?

Healing is the inherent capacity of life. It is the organism's ability to mend itself. By nature, it functions toward homeostasis, a state of internal balance. Healing arises from the internal nature of DNA, the original blueprint of life. Within DNA rests all information needed to manufacture enzymes for repair. Our healing system continually operates of its own volition.

Natural Healing Is Rediscovered in our Time by the Medical Profession

Scientific research on the role of the mind and imagination in promoting health is called psycho-neuro-immunology. It is one of the most exciting fields of research today. Although the mind's key role in inducing changes in the organism has been researched scientifically in psychotherapy and the behavioral sciences for some time, it has only lately begun to attract medical research attention

Psychologist Dr. Lawrence LeShan linked emotions to cancer in his pioneering studies in the 1950s. He theorized that unexpressed trauma in a child's mind may induce disease in later years[7]. In the nineteen seventies, Dr. Carl Simonton and Dr. Stephanie Matthews' research on imaging techniques in the treatment of cancer patients was a scientific breakthrough. It gave credibility to the science of mind and body medicine and this new field attracted the attention of the medical establishment. In 1975, Dr. Simonton's study of over 152 cancer patients showed that the twenty patients who responded very well to their treatment had in common a positive attitude and a strong belief system[8].

Dr. Norman Cousins' book *The Healing Heart*[9] offers evidence of the role of the imagination in cases of remarkable recovery. A profile of the exceptional patient who defies the odds by recovering or developing unusual immunity in the midst of crippling disease starts to form. Dr. Cousins identifies an exceptional patient as one who can laugh. Fear and stress, two factors that lower the immune system, are dissolved with the ability to enjoy another side of life.

---

[7] *Quantum Healing*, p.32. Deepak Chopra, MD. Bantam New Age Books 1989.
[8] *Creating Health*, p.22. Deepak Chopra. Houghton Mifflin Company, Boston 1987.
[9] *The Healing Heart*. Norman Cousins.

In a landmark study *Imagery in Healing* [10] funded by the National Cancer Institute, Jeanne Achterberg identifies a second type of exceptional cancer patient. In the research, all patients received the same cancer treatment- surgery followed by a mild form of chemotherapy. One group of patients was encouraged to turn to an outside source of support for renewed strength, such as a person, church or job. Patients in a second group were helped to heighten their psychological awareness. In both cases, the patients who did well were the ones who could rally a positive attitude and take an active part in reversing the course of the disease.

Over a three-year period, psychologist Michael Lerner conducted an in-depth study of forty clinics offering alternative approaches to treating cancer[11]. He interviewed patients who visualized positive images and followed herbal and macrobiotics diets. Forty percent believed they had experienced a temporary improvement in the quality of their lives. Forty percent experienced actual medical improvements in their condition lasting from a few days to a number of years. Ten percent said they got nothing out of the treatment and the other ten percent felt they had partially or totally recovered from the disease.

The intricacy of mind-body relations in treatment is not easily ascertained through research and many of these results have been contested. We understand now that a disease, especially in the case of cancer, a malfunction at the level of cellular activity,

---

10   *Imagery in Healing*, Jeanne Achterberg. Shambhala Boston and London 1985.
11   *Quantum Healing*. Deepak Chopra. MD. p.29. Batam Books 1990.

has multiple causes and the "risk factors" are many. Nevertheless, every practicing physician knows that the patient's will to recover plays a fundamental role in her or his treatment.

Spontaneous Remission

The first World Conference on spontaneous remission from cancer took place in 1974 at Johns Hopkins University School of Medicine. A major study using medical library resources by Eric Peper and Ken Pelletier [12] reported about four hundred spontaneous remissions from cancer. Elmer and Alyce Green of the Menninger Clinic determined that all the patients had one thing in common. They all had cultivated a strong, hopeful attitude before their remission occurred. Sometimes a spontaneous remission will happen without a change of heart or mind. What happens is that the body's remarkable intelligence is functioning all the time.

The Placebo Effect

Placebo comes from the Latin verb placere to please. In medical terms, a placebo is a substance devoid of an active therapeutic element. In control studies, a placebo is used to test the effectiveness of a drug. One group of patients is given the experimental drug, the other is given a placebo. The placebo effect is the term for the change that occurs in the absence of medical intervention. It is tangible proof of the role the

---

12   Ibid, p.169.

imagination plays in inducing a positive reaction. The response triggered by a placebo demonstrates the electrochemical effect that a conscious thought produces. This can be seen effectively in the case of pain. When placebos are administered, the body has the ability to increase its production of endorphins. The trigger is not in the sugar pill or in the water, but in the belief or faith of the recipient. Thirty to seventy percent of all healing through drug and surgical intervention has been ascribed to the placebo effect.

Norman Cousins offers a very significant comment on the use of placebos: "What is most significant about placebos is not so much the verdict they supply on the efficacy of new drugs, as the clear proof that what passes through the mind can produce alterations in the body's chemistry."[13]

However, a positive attitude as planned therapy has limited success unless we go deep into the field of silent intelligence: a field below our objective mind where, in the silence of our heart, we become attuned to the great mystery of life.

Healing and the Human Spirit

Many dramatic healings of the sick have been attributed to prayers and faith. During a state of ecstasy, trance or sleep, or when emotions make a quantum leap, a cure can take place. On the other hand, negative beliefs and fears can inhibit the

---

[13] Ibid, p. 86.

process. This was known in aboriginal societies and in antiquity. For example, the temple of Aesculapius, the Greek God of healing, was filled with sleepers who were visited by the god in their sleep at the suggestion of priests, and miraculous cures followed. Dr. P.P. Quimby[14], the founder of spiritual and mental healing science in the nineteenth century and the father of the "New Thought Movement," practiced his healing art in the belief that the human spirit possesses senses or powers that function independently of matter. One of his patients and followers was Mrs. Mary Baker Eddy, the founder of Christian Science. Dr. Quimby believed that the imagination is the most powerful faculty of the human mind and he based his cures on it.

Miraculous Healing

For over one hundred and seventy years, people from all parts of the world have come to believe in the miraculous power of the waters in Lourdes, France. There it is said that the Virgin Mary appeared to Bernadette Soubirou in 1858. As noted earlier, the belief in Mary the mother of God has been often accompanied by blessings, ecstasies, and healing. In most cases, the healing occurs at a very fast rate. It shows an acceleration of the normal processes of organic repair. Crutches, wheelchairs, braces and protheses no longer needed are on display at Lourdes. These are testimonials to the healings that have occurred.

---

14   *The Quimby Manuscripts*. The Citadel Press 1980.

Healing is an Ancient Art

In ancient times, initiated priests of mystery schools in Egypt, Greece and elsewhere were sought out as doctors. Their knowledge came from observing the nature of plants, minerals and animals as well as the sky and the revolution of planets. We know that the Chaldean and Mayan astrologers observed the sky over several millennia. They gained a reverence for the unfathomable depth of time with an understanding of cosmic cycles. From their accumulated observations came a wealth of practical knowledge and insight into the human being's double nature as a child of the Cosmos and of the earth. These ancient priests saw the human body as a miniature of the Universe. In their view, the body was the house of the soul which reflected the Cosmos. Healing the soul was to heal the body. Medicine therefore became a branch of religion.

The Ancient Knowledge Within Us

I remember closing my eyes as a child before going to sleep and being swept into a world of cosmic grandeur and beauty. Swirls of stars of all colors and brightness would pass in spiral formation as if on a three-dimensional movie screen inside my head. This breathtaking spectacle was on display just for me, and every night I waited eagerly to be airlifted on my journey among the stars. Was I born with a little bit of the old memory? Were the stellar heavens really home?

I believe we are born with seed knowledge of our spiritual origin. Buried deep inside our being, like the flower's seed in the furrow of a wintry earth, our spiritual light awaits germination. But unlike the flower that unfurls its unique beauty at springtime, nature has not by itself led human nature to its unique destiny. As our senses and intellect have developed, we have lost the knowledge of our divine nature. We vacillate between the pull of the earth and the call of the stars. Sensual attachment blurs the memory of our stellar origins. Could the price entail the loss of our soul?

Since the dawn of time, revelation of our spiritual origin has been available. Time and again, humanity lost the memory and reneged on the responsibility to live accordingly. In the light of the new Millennium, we see a need for change. Social, political, and ethical structures are being challenged. Some of us look back in dismay, wondering where it all went wrong. Others like me look at these symptoms with great hope and, instead of decay, see the emergence of the new.

Both star beings and earthlings, human beings have a unique position in the Universe. With our own free will, we can retrieve our cosmic heritage. Healers see themselves as beings of light dancing with life, as co-creators with the great power of Love-in-the-making, the Divine Intelligence that operates in the Universe we call God. We are here on this planet to evolve in consciousness of our spiritual heritage. To grow into self-knowledge and use our newfound power wisely.

AN OVERVIEW
Sacred Knowledge

From time immemorial knowledge was transmitted orally. The science of the spirit or sacred science's origins stretch beyond recorded history. Its sources lie in the oral and written traditions of Mesopotamia, the ancient texts of India, the Mosaic Kabbalah, the Buddhist texts, the sacred traditions of ancient Egypt, the Holy Scriptures of the Bible, the Koran, and the New Testament. We find this tradition alive in the myths and legends of Homer and the Greek bards, in Celtic folk tales, and those of all aboriginal cultures around the world as Joseph Campbell [15] so successfully demonstrated. All traditions originate with the story of a golden age, a time when the gods or God were revealed to humankind. There is a singular unity of design that seems to point to a common origin.

Mystery Schools and Rites

The memory of humanity's divine nature was kept alive from archaic times in centers of worship, also centers of learning. Herodotus, the first known historian of Greek origin, mentions mystery rites in Egypt and Greece in these words: "the proceedings of these ceremonies will not pass my lips."[16] The word "Mysteria" in Ancient Greece designated a festi-

---

15   Joseph Campbell. *The Masks of God: Creative Mythology*. Penguin Books, 1976.
16   *The History of Herodotus, Book II* p.142. Tudor Publishing Company, N.Y.1941.

val filled with sacred events and rites[17]. These festivals were distinguished between lesser and greater mysteries, the lesser pertaining to our human nature, the greater to the divine. In the divine centers of Greek Mysteries an uplifting atmosphere was evoked which touched both the senses and the spirit.

Initiation

Initio means going into a new beginning. To participate in the Mysteries, one had to be initiated. The experience was of an ineffable nature. It was unutterable and not to be revealed. The goal of the initiation was to attune the physical or small ego with the spiritual essence believed to be the real Self. Only then could the microcosm or human being reflect the macrocosm or Divine nature. As above, so below.

Secrecy

In the Mystery Schools of Egypt and Greece, tradition was enshrined in the utmost secrecy so as to preserve against superstition and idolatry. Once uttered, precious wisdom may have become commonplace. Locked within allegories it was revealed so the ones who had ears could hear to perfect their internal spiritual faculties. For instance, one of the Fathers of the Church, Origen of Alexandria (184-254 AD), admitted "to the literal mind we teach the Gospel in the historic way, but to the proficient we impart the Logos, the word of God".

---

17 *The Mysteries. Paper* from The Eranos Yearbooks edited by Joseph Campbell. Princeton/Bollingen Paperback 1978.

In the Mysteries was taught the truth of primitive revelation, the existence of One Great Invisible God, eternal and infinite, the source of all things. Four thousand years ago, knowledge of the immortality of the soul was kept alive by Egyptian high priests. They saw the soul as a divine spark expanding toward its own cause, the indwelling eternal Good. The ultimate goal was to attain a level of consciousness each time higher until the ultimate reunion with the divine essence was achieved. During the initiation ceremony, the great verities by which the Universe is identified with that one divine essence were revealed. The experience was meant to induce a profound change, an opening of new consciousness so that mere beliefs gave way to knowledge. Not only did the initiates receive keys to their salvation, but with them came the revelation of the nature of the mind and its power over matter. Only one with a pure heart could be entrusted to receive such power. An old adage says: When the student is ready, the Master appears. Sacred Science is not readily available unless one is searching for it.

Esoteric and Exoteric Path

Every great religion has an esoteric tradition or inner way and an exoteric tradition or outer way to redemption.

Esoteric means not publicly disclosed, confidential, intended for or understood by only a small group. It also means difficult to understand, abstruse. The esoteric path is one of personal commitment and dedication to self-knowledge. The eternal and universal approach to self-knowledge is through the path of union, "I and the Father are One" called the inner way. Students stand all alone, a position not without danger, for they are being tested and are subject to vacillations. A preparation involving steps of purification is required of the neophyte before the secret doctrine can be confided. Trust is required on this path. In the esoteric tradition, the one power or God is experienced as immanent in its own creation. We are one with the source in whom we live and have our being. The esoteric path is the one followed by mystics, saints, gurus and holy people the world over.

Exoteric means pertaining to the outside or external, comprehensible or suited to the public, that which is popular. The exoteric path demands a certain degree of obedience to teachings based on revelation or myths interpreted by selected few and duly recorded into dogma or Law. It is hierarchical by nature as the leader has authority over the believer. In our western tradition we have the metaphor of the Good Shepherd leading his sheep to salvation. Scholars and Doctors of the Law become the ultimate arbiters on the road to salvation and ask their followers to show obedience and faith in their leadership. Arbiters of this path need to demonstrate purity of heart and mind otherwise the letter of the law could be substituted for its substance.

Both esoteric and exoteric paths share the same belief. One is the inner, the other the outer way. One sees the truth as the One power immanent in its own creation, we are all part of it. The other sees the truth as the supreme power transcending time and space, creator of all things apart from and beyond creation, a power outside of self. Both paths present inherent dangers and both can lead to illumination. To describe the exoteric and the esoteric path we may look at the Temple of Jerusalem as a metaphor. The mass of people had free access inside the first court. To enter the second court, one had to perform the ritual of purification. But to enter the inner sanctuary or Tabernacle and look behind the veil, the "Holy of Holies," one had to be initiated. No one else could behold the vision.

The way of the healer is the inner way. To become a healer, transformation has to happen from inside.

Spirituality and Religion

What is the difference between spirituality and religion? Spirituality is concerned or based on the immaterial aspect of existence. The word spirit as opposed to matter means the animating or vital principle of a person, animal or nature. A spiritual life is a commitment to search beyond appearances toward union with our divine essence. We do not need to belong to a church to lead a spiritual life.

A religion embraces a particular system of faith based on revelation within the culture that gave its birth. A religion's aim is the spiritual guidance and indoctrination of its faithful. When we follow the spirit of the Law whatever our religion, we are one with God. If we accept the word and miss the substance, we remain imperfect and unenlightened. Religions tend to become powerful organizations with their own set of rules that have in the past generated mutual distrust. The hope for the future is to see all religions bonded in mutual tolerance and unconditional love with no dictates whatsoever to infringe on the freedom of each individual. To each his or her own.

UNIVERSAL PRINCIPLES

Duality and Unity

The Judeo-Christian tradition created a distinction between body and soul based on the works of the Greek philosopher Aristoteles. In the Christian tradition, which influenced western culture, the body was seen as impure, the root cause of all evil. Centuries of neglecting the body to save the soul led to a dichotomy, the mind on the one side and the body on the other. The system of value that follows this concept is based on right and wrong.

The Buddhist tradition in the East sees the senses as unreliable: not in any way evil but maya or illusion. The world seen through our five senses is not the real world. Behind the veil of illusion stands the real world that is one of unity. Buddhist philosophy is based on non-attachment, in which desire is seen as the source of all suffering. The return to Oneness or unity is through the practice of meditation with the realization that all creation is a manifestation of the One spirit or God. Through compassion and service, one partakes of the spirit that underlies all life.

Eastern Way, Western Way

Let's go back to fundamentals. The Eastern religious tradition is based on the principle of oneness and multiplicity. The world is seen as coming from one source and all parts are a manifestation of the Oneness of all things. There is no separation. The Buddha teaches Oneness or serenity through non-attachment. Suffering is a consequence of desire and brought about by the illusion that the world as our senses see it, is all there is.

The Western religious tradition is based on the belief of one Divine creator separated from his creation. Alienated from God, we view creation as both good and bad. In this view, there is separation from oneness into duality. Good and evil divide human nature. The struggle is on at all times; the victory of one side means the defeat of the other.

Holistic View

This view offers an alternative of hope. Body and mind merge as two aspects of the same vital energy. On what foundation does this later view rests? Rudolf Steiner, the German philosopher and admirer of Goethe whose phenomenal vision as a scientist and metaphysician took root in the nineteenth century, saw human beings as potential stabilizers between the forces of good and evil. The model he has for human beings is that of the Resurrected Christ in its cosmic splendor, a Christ that is close to the messianic view of the Essenes and Gnostic sects. In Steiner's view, Christ exemplifies the light of the world, the redeemed spirit of humanity, the fallen Adam, the Buddha in creation, the core, the center revealed to itself. To recognize our spiritual nature, that of the Christ within working through the duality of our body-mind relationship is to restore the point of balance, the source of our wholeness and our healing power.

A LITTLE BIT OF HISTORY

The Plurality of Gods in the Religions of Antiquity

Religious traditions go back in time beyond any recorded history. To alleviate fear and rekindle hope, human beings have from time immemorial turned to the heavens for help. In scrutinizing the stars and observing natural phenomena, they have hoped to temper elemental forces.

The pantheon of Gods displayed in ancient religions like Hinduism were a function of practical life. The Godhead Brahma was believed too transcendent, too remote in the Cosmos to interfere with people's problems. The worship of local deities provided for the village's welfare. The exalted aspect of worship became confused with secular manipulation. Egyptian High priests were more sophisticated. They understood the reality of abstract thinking. They conceived of functions or powers (Plato called them archetypes) to which they gave the name of "Neter". These powers preside over specific activities and derive from the one eternal and infinite God who has made all things, who begetteth but was never begotten [18]. Neter provides a pantheon of many Gods to be worshiped not as personalities but only for the functions they represent. Similarly, Rudolf Steiner saw formative forces at work behind every aspect of creation to be called upon as divine essences[19].

The Development of Western Culture

The history of Western culture in Europe since the Renaissance in the 15th century illustrates the growing independence of individuals from the considerable power of the Roman Catholic Church. Scientific observations became favored over religious dogmas. This eventually resulted in freeing the thinking mind from the control of the Church and giving free rein to the growth of the intellect. What was believed with religious fervor in the Middle Ages could no longer be proven rationally. Freeing the intellect was a correction from superstitions and from the centralization of power whether exerted by the

---

[18] *The Egyptian Book of The Dead.* E. A. Wallis Budge. Dover Publications, Inc. New York 1987.

[19] *Knowledge of The Higher Worlds and its Attainment.* Rudolf Steiner. Anthroposophic Press, Inc. 1947.

church, family, or state. In the 17th century, the Age of Reason followed. The French philosopher Descartes illustrated the ultimate affirmation of the individual for generations to come with his, "Je pense, donc je suis." "I think, therefore I am."

The nineteenth century focused on scientific discoveries. Science became the new religion, scientists the new gods. Progress offered the key to utopia, the Promised Land, freedom from all contingencies, and solutions to all riddles of the mind. By the same token it justified greed and a drive for power in the delusion that people like systems ought to be controlled. The Industrial Revolution was born and so was our materialistic society.

At the beginning of the 21st century, we are now coming full circle. Leaving behind a mechanistic view of the universe based on Newtonian physics, we discover a new worldview with the help of Quantum Physics. Now we see all creation as pure energy, as all is interconnected. The earth is no longer a machine invented by a great engineer, but rather, as the ancients understood, a living entity[20]. We have a responsible role to play in this intelligent universe. No longer separate, we're part of the cosmic whole. What awaits us is a higher level of consciousness as we move on the evolutionary spiral. It is the ultimate challenge. How can we be true to our Self?

---

20 *Discordant Harmonies*. Daniel B. Botkin. Oxford University Press, Inc. 1990.

SACRED SCIENCE

The Quest

Sacred Science or spiritual science is the quest for the infinite power that sustains all life. It is based on the realization that all creation emanates from one divine Power. From that one source comes all life. In our quest, we find inspiration in both Eastern and Western esoteric traditions.

The Eastern Esoteric Tradition

Perhaps the most ancient scriptures to reveal our divine origin come from the land of India. For over three thousand years, there has existed a Sanskrit culture that emerged from an unwritten language called Aryan shared among people in the Indus Valley. The most ancient part of the texts, the Rig-Veda, was compiled from Vedic hymns, legends and stories that show the origin of the worship of fire in the rites. In it there is a song of Creation that praises the highest heavens when humanity was one with God. The development of spiritual wisdom is reflected in the sacred texts of the Upanishads with their epic tale of the Mahabharata that includes the beautiful philosophical poem of the Bhagavad-Gita[21]. The latter poem focuses on spiritual liberation in the form of a dialogue between the god

---

21   *The Bhagavad Gita*. Translated by Juan Mascaro. Penguins Books, 1962.

Krishna (the charioteer) and the warrior Arjuna, a dialogue that is resolved by mystical union with the One.

The vision of The Gita has inspired many philosophers, poets and readers of all kinds since it was first translated into English. Both Emerson and Thoreau were familiar with it. It inspired Thoreau's retreat in search of inner illumination. It also inspired the poet T.S. Elliot to write one of the most profound poems in English literature "The Four Quartets"[22]. Out of this Eastern tradition, there emerged over centuries a very practical system known as Yoga or union with the Source. This practice relies on reflection on the nature of the mind and the necessity to train it through both physical and spiritual practices. It gave birth to several religious movements, including Buddhism and Taoism, both rooted in Hinduism. These movements share the concept of "Dharma" which means universal law or the right way of living. Both share the principle of "Tao," the oneness behind all creation that we can sense through our inner reality[23].

The Western Esoteric Tradition

The Western esoteric tradition is based in part on the mystic tradition of saints like Saint Teresa of Avila, Saint John of the Cross and Saint Francis of Assisi who advocate "union with God" through prayers, poverty, and chastity and on the

---
22   *Four Quartets*. T.S. Elliot. Faber & Faber, London 1969.
23   *Tao. The Chinese Philosophy of Time and Change*. Philip Rawson and Laszlo Legeza. Thames and Hudson Ltd. London 1973.

ancient tradition of Jewish mysticism or Kabbalah. Judaism is the matrix of two more religions, Christianity and Islam. These three religions are based on what the Koran calls the "Book" that includes the Torah and the Bible. Kabbalah is the mystical path in Judaism. It has its source in the ancient land of Mesopotamia whose rich culture was open to Zoroaster's mysticism and monotheism, the science of the Magi, and ancient Egyptian mysteries.

The ancient Egyptians had a vision of humanity transcending physical reality. The Book of the Dead meticulously records all the different layers of being that in their view constitutes the whole person. Besides the soul were other elements that would rise to life again after death. These layers consisted of a natural body, a spiritual body, a heart, a double, a shadow, an intangible ethereal casing or spirit, a form and a name. All these were bound inseparably and made human beings' part heavenly and part earthly. The heart was the seat of life's power and the source of good and evil thoughts. Through prayers and ceremonies, the physical body called "Khat" was transformed into a spiritual body "sahu." Wholeness was the goal. It reflected the divine Cosmos. The myth of Osiris and Isis was not only a cult to bring fertility to the land but a way to represent the immortal part of Humanity. It was an inspiration and symbol of death and resurrection. Little do we realize how much the Egyptians contributed to the Christian belief in the immortality of the soul and resurrection after death!

Kabbalah

The word in Hebrew means "receiving tradition". Kabbalah is a set of esoteric teachings meant to explain the relationship between an unchanging, eternal, and mysterious Ein Sof (no end) and the mortal and finite universe (God's creation). The Kabbalah's occult tradition originates from the second Temple (6th century BC) and is based on the prophetic vision of Ezechiel. The root of its system is the Tree of Life, which acts as a meditation symbol. It consists of ten Divine Emanations or Sephirots which are arranged on the tree of Life as a structure of twenty-two paths, the same number as the Hebrew alphabet[24].

Hebrew is a sacred language. It is to the western esoteric tradition what Sanskrit is for the eastern tradition. Its esoteric wisdom is based on the science of numbers as each letter in the Hebrew alphabet relates to one number. The sum of the numbers represented by each letter within a word adds a symbolic value to its discursive meaning. This process is called Gematria. It is an intricate system that can unravel the relationships of cosmic factors and can enshrine great truths. Kabbalah's system of notation is the basis of ceremonial magic with its names of power and the Tarot system of divination.

Sufism

Sufism or tasawwuf in Arabic is recognized to be the mystic or psycho-spiritual dimension of Islam. Seyyed Hossein Nasr,

---

[24] *The Mystical Qabalah*. Dion Fortune. Samuel Weiser, Inc. 1984.

one of the most recognized researchers affirms that Islam is the name of the inner mystical way. The essence of the ritual in Sufism is simple. The Sufi initiate abandons himself/herself to God's love at each moment of his/her life. Sufism is the spiritual journey toward knowledge of God. To express all the states of consciousness along the different levels, Sufis have produced throughout the centuries an abundant literature. In the same way that each Moslem expresses his/her faith to reach the knowledge of God after death and the final judgment in Paradise, Sufi saints think that it is possible to know and experience the love of God while here on earth. S/he sees in creation God's final goal.

Man qaala laa ilaaha ill Allah, dakhala al-janna
Who says, there is only God as God, will enter Paradise

Hadith of the Prophet Muhammad

In the *Hadith qudsi*, we find:

"I was a hidden treasure and my desire was to be known, this is why I created the world."

Among the many mystics and scholars which this ancient tradition has offered the world, Djalâ-Od-Dîn Rûmî is one of the great figures. He is the founder of the order of the Whirling Dervishes whose dancing symbolizes the round of the planets around the sun and whose music awakens the mysteries of the heart. A 13th century thinker who was already writing about the plurality of solar systems and atom fission, his poetry the RUBÂI'ÂT is considered one of the most beautiful poems of universal literature. These small poems are nuances of the different spiritual states, from love for the beloved to love of one's union with a sacred cosmos through the awakening of the heart.

Alchemy

The school of Alexandria was a breeding ground for Neo-Platonists and had a tremendous impact on medieval esotericism. Its philosophy was greatly influenced by the art of alchemy, the transforming of gross matter into a finer spirit or elixir. Mircea Eliade (Parabola, volume 3 No. 3- The Myth of Alchemy) writes that in almost every ancient culture we find Alchemy and it is almost always related to a mystical esoteric tradition. Alchemy may have its source in Egypt (AL-KHEMY means red earth). Its origin was attributed to Hermes Trismegistus or "Thrice Great", considered the "Master of Masters" of ancient Egypt. He was said to have the attributes of Thoth the Egyptian God of wisdom and Hermes, messenger of the Gods in the Greek pantheon. Fragments of his teachings or hermetic philosophy are found in the "Kybalion"[25] and reveal a fountain of wisdom. In all traditions, esoteric alchemical doctrines and techniques were transmitted secretly. The alchemical process comprises an initiation and a series of specific expe-

---

25   *The Kybalion*. The Yogi Publication Society, Masonic Temple. Chicago, Illinois 1940.

riences towards the radical transformation of the human condition that includes longevity and immortality as well as transformation of base metal into gold.

The Mystic Way

Saint John of the Cross wrote eloquently in his work "The Dark Night of the Soul", a spiritually moving journey towards divine union with God. A poet at heart, St John uses a beautiful, rich, symbolic language and his "Ascent to Mount Carmel" and "Spiritual Canticle of the Soul" are among the most profound works of Christian mysticism. St Teresa of Avila, his contemporary, experienced ecstatic visions while in the Carmelite order where she came to endure Christ's Passion. She wrote the "Way of Perfection" and the "Interior Castle" where she shows the way toward union with God through prayers, meditations and silence. St Francis of Assisi was a man who astounded and inspired the Catholic Church by taking the gospels literally, joyfully, and humbly. He led a life of devotion and care for the poor. He is considered the Patron Saint of animals as he came to understand their language and embrace the whole of creation in his love of God. His "Cantico del Frate Sole "is a hymn to the sun, moon, stars, wind, fire, air, and earth. All creatures and the earth and heavens are one with God.

Language

A common language had to be found that could speak to the soul as well as the mind. Legends, fables, myths and symbols could preserve the essence of sacred knowledge. But what could appeal directly to the intellect as well as the intuition was the language of numbers. Through numbers we unlock the secrets of our relationship to the Universe. Sacred science is revealed through the meaning of numbers.

Pythagoras

The science of mathematics inspired the Greek philosopher Pythagoras with higher wisdom. He saw in numbers the structure of the Universe and the genesis of ideas. Geometry for him was the key to the Divine and our true nature. Numbers represented the formative forces behind all creation in their interrelationship to the whole. Pythagoras's ideas inspired among others the Freemasons whose secret society takes as a model the legend of King Solomon sending for King Hiram and the building of the temple of Jerusalem. Their tradition is based on harmony and measures within numbers. God is the Great Architect of the Universe who has for symbols the compass and the square. Redemption is the rebuilding of the new Temple on earth, a metaphor for human beings' transformation through harmony and measure.

From Measure and Proportions Come Beauty and Harmony

A simple pattern of numbers guides the form of living things. Plants in their evolution follow a mathematical blueprint called the Fibonacci Series named after a mathematician Leonardo Pisano known as Fibonacci in Medieval Europe[26]. In that sequence, every number after the first two is the sum of the two preceding ones.

Fibonacci had discovered a general law of aesthetics and beauty. The Ancient Greeks already knew this universal measure of beauty which they learnt from the Egyptians. They called it the "golden section", or "golden mean" or "phi", nature's greatest secret. It defines the shape and structure of many living organisms as well as the spirals of galaxies that develop according to the Fibonacci numbers. The ancient Greek temples including the Parthenon are based on a measure of the golden mean. They have conveyed through the ages a feeling of beauty and harmony. This law of growth affects not only plants but also the rabbit population, the family tree of bees, stock market patterns, the self-organizing DNA nucleotides, as well as the shape of a mollusk's shell.

Throughout the Middle Ages architecture was considered a sacred art that reflected the ultimate meaning of life. Medieval cathedrals were oriented according to the light and the four cardinal points as the School of Chartres (11-12th centuries) illustrates. The shape of cathedrals incorporated all forms and levels of spatial geometry. Based on right measures and proportions, these forms and planes gave birth to a sense of beauty, harmony and heightened consciousness. For the Master Mason, the cube, the sphere and the triangle had sacred meanings. Symbols whose esoteric knowledge were known

---

26 *Sacred Geometry*. Robert Lawlor. Thames and Hudson Ltd. London, 1982.

only to the "Guilds" or the Fraternity of Masons were secretly guarded and carved into the stone so knowledge could be kept alive without interfering with religious dogma.

The Guilds of masons who built the cathedrals in the Middle Ages were formed for the continuity of the craft. Information relating to the art was kept secret only to be passed to master masons. It was an open book for those who understood that there was a spiritual message locked in the stone not always acceptable to the orthodoxy of the church. The key was revealed through numbers to those who had been initiated.

NUMBERS

What Can Numbers Reveal?

Numbers have a symbolic meaning beyond their numerical value. They are representative of forces interacting with each other. Let us examine the numbers one to ten called generative numbers. These ten digits are contained within the tetractys or Pythagoras's sacred number.

What is their Message?

One
One or the Monad is represented by the circle. It is the beginning of all things and as such represents unity out of which all creation proceeds. One represents un-polarized energy. Being

the source, one is un-begotten. It reveals our concept of God or the One or Universal Mind as the seed that holds all life. One is only divisible by itself. Multiply one, you will always find the number one. For that reason, "One" represents divinity. It is the alpha and the omega, the beginning and the end. Multiplicity is created out of Unity.

Two

Two represents the descent of spirit into matter. When the One becomes manifest on the plane of form, it enters the realm of duality. The number two conveys the principle of polarity with its law of opposites, feminine and masculine. In sacred geometry if we draw a straight line from both sides of a point, we have two lines that lead in opposite directions. Since there are no straight lines in the universe both ends will meet again, bringing to life the principle of Yin and Yang, the masculine and feminine aspects that together form the One or the unity of all life! The number two represents the principle of cell division. Each daughter cell is identical to the mother cell.

Three

Since ancient times, the number three has been the symbol of divinity in the mystery of creation. In sacred science the number three represents the concept of the whole larger than the sum of its parts and 1+1 equals 3 as the intercourse of two elements produces a third element. Many religions incorporate the principle of the triangle to represent the threefold aspect of divinity.

The Christian Church is founded on the Trinity, a symbol of the three aspects of God in One: The Father principle, the Holy Spirit as the agent of manifestation and the Son as God revealed in matter. In Hinduism, Brahma the Universal One who represents the Superior World is the first person of the creative Triad, Vishnu is the Divine Spirit pervading all creation, Shiva the Lord of the Dance is the third aspect representing the inferior world or the world of change. In the Egyptian Mysteries, the Myth of Divinity is represented by the legend of Osiris God-King, Isis Goddess of earth and fecundity and Horus son of Isis and Osiris, symbol of the new germ of life.

Four

The number four is the symbol of the Earth. The earth is represented by the square. There are four cardinal points and four corners of the earth. In our earthy nature we offer four temperaments: melancholy, phlegm, choler and sanguinity. The ancient Greeks found that all matter is composed of four elements: air, water, fire and earth. In the spiritual realm the number four represents illumination and the Kabbalah teaches the four worlds of illumination. In Jewish mysticism the divine name of God is represented by four letters Yod-He-Vau-He, Yaveh, also called the Tetragrammaton. The four cherubs guarded the Temple of Salomon, four goddesses guarded the tomb of Tutankhamun, and four rivers flowed out of the

Garden of Eden. Beyond the third dimension of time and space lies the fourth dimension of pure consciousness.

Five

The number five is associated with change for the good or bad. The fifth day is crucial in the development of disease where a change can come for the better or worse. Five is at the center of a series of ten that represents unity in its wholeness. Leonardo da Vinci drew a man within a circle whose outstretched arms and legs and erect head formed a pentagram. This is the vision of the newly born in spirit represented by the number 5. Over the cave of the heart of the evolving consciousness of humanity called the Spirit Self, the pentagon or five-pointed star hovers above the newborn infant and its symbol is the star of Bethlehem.

Six

The number six represents harmony between the spiritual and the material world. Two triangles intermingle, one points upward, the other downward. Together they form the six-pointed star of Solomon's seal reflecting the human and the divine in a working partnership of harmony and equilibrium. The achievement is through the elevation of the human to the Divine level. Six is a building number. In the Book of Genesis, creation was completed in six days. God saw that the work was good and prepared for a rest or Sabbath on the seventh day. Six represents preparation and purification.

Seven

Seven represents rest, completion. After the six days of creation, seven represents perfection. It is the number that corresponds to complete manifestation combining the spiritual factor of three with the material factor of four. It represents the complete working of involution and evolution, the spiritual and the material that together constitute the whole.

Eight

The figure eight describes two equal loops that meet at a center point. It holds the secret to equilibrium as the power of polarity is contained within it. It is the highest feminine number in the entire series and represents intuition. It is the number of regenerations, as its vibratory power tends to lift one beyond the limitations of personal environment. In the musical scale, the eighth note is the beginning of a new octave. Eight is the symbol of the resurrection into a new consciousness. Old baptisteries were octagonal as a symbol of the new birth. In the Jewish tradition, a child is circumcised after eight days.

Nine

The number nine means foundation and symmetry. It is symbolized by three triangles which represent the divine, the human and the underworld in perfect balance in its threefold aspects of soul, body and spirit. The number nine resists destruction, keeping its own identity through any numeral combination. It always returns to itself. When nine is multiplied by another number, it always reproduces itself. Nine is the number guiding human evolution. The child is born after nine months of gestation. So close to number ten, which represents unity in consciousness, nine symbolizes the whole on its way to integration. Nine is the number of mankind in generation. The neo-Platonists saw ninefold hierarchies (angels, archangels, archai, exousia, dynameis, kyriotes. thrones, cherubim, and seraphim) forming the ascending path of spiritual development.

Ten

Ten is the number of humanities in regeneration. It is Pythagoras' sacred number. Pythagoras arranged the number ten or tetractys in a pyramidal form with one digit on top, two digits underneath, three below and four at the base. Ten contains all formative principles as it contains all numbers and returns to one. In the beginning is the end. The tetractys represents unity manifested through multiplicity and is the key to harmony that governs creation. It is the number from which all things have come, and into which all things must return. The Law was written in stone into Ten Commandments. In the Kabbalah "ten" is the all-embracing number.

All numbers up to ten are formative numbers. After ten numbers are combinations of the fundamental ones.

Summary

Before Aristotle opened the path to objective consciousness, medicine and religion were entwined. To heal the soul was to heal the body. From time immemorial, the memory of our divine essence was preserved. Each great religion has its part in the transmission of sacred knowledge based on revelation. They share a common ground in the belief of one Supreme intelligence or God creator of the universe. Their differences lie mostly in the interpretation of the revelation. The exoteric path is the outer way to salvation through adherence to religious principles or laws. The esoteric path is the inner way to union with the Godhead. We do not need the stamp of a religious affiliation to develop our cosmic maturity although every religion offers the guidance needed. In the 21st century it is time to deepen our self-knowledge and participate in the development of a new consciousness to actualize our cosmic inheritance.

CHAPTER TWO

KNOW THYSELF

"No Law can be Sacred to me but that of my own Nature"
¬Ralph Waldo Emerson, *Self- Reliance*

In the Mystery Schools, one of the great truths revealed was the threefold nature of human beings. The macrocosm reflected in the microcosm its threefold divine aspects. The former was represented by the upper triangle, the later by the lower triangle. When they merge together we have Solomon's seal. As above, so below. Let's look at this mysterious being that we are. What do we see?

Microcosm

We have a threefold nature of mind, body, and soul. It operates through centers within the body that are all related by way of a network of glands and nervous plexuses called the endocrine system. These three centers are:

The head seat of the intellect.
The heart seat of the soul.
The abdomen seat of instinct.

Threefold in our human nature, we operate as one microcosm within the macrocosmic universe.

Macrocosm

In the Veda Scriptures, the three aspects of God's consciousness are revealed unfolded in human nature:

Vishnu the Divine in its many incarnations is represented as located in the head.

Brahma the One Omnipresent and eternal is seen as the pulse in the heart.

Shiva the preserver and destroyer in nature is seen as seated in the abdomen.

The Emergence of The New Self

Nature endows us with all the physical faculties needed for life on this planet. Our human organism contains elements of all the other kingdoms, vegetal, mineral and animal. Throughout its nine months of gestation, the human fetus recaptures all the steps of its evolution from the one-cell amoebae to the more complex creature which took nature eons to perfect. Above and beyond our physical evolution as a human race, the soul stirring within us demands to come out to renew its connection with the divine source. The next stage of evolution is the development of our mental and spiritual power. It involves free will and the decision is up to us.

The Body as a Temple

Our soul is wrapped up in the garment of our body. If our soul is holy why not consider our body as a sacred temple? Temples in antiquity and medieval Cathedrals developed their shape according to a canon of harmony based on numbers and orientation in space[27]. In his book "The Temple of Man" the French-Alsatian writer Shwaller de Lubicz dedicated most of his adult life to the study of the Temple of Luxor in Egypt. Shwaller saw in Luxor the representation of the body of man in generic terms revealing through its architectural structure

---

27   *The Gothic Cathedral.* Otto von Simson. Bollingen Series/Princeton 1956.

the ultimate transformation that will take place when enlightenment comes.

Architecture is a Visual as Well as a Spatial Experience

Vitruvius, a Roman writer and expert on architecture, warned in his own time (100 BC) that an architect without knowledge of anatomy could not build a house well! The human frame is poised in space inwardly and outwardly. Have you ever reflected that you function in a three-dimensional space? In its three-dimensional space your human skeleton is like a monument with height, width and length.

Symbols Within the Body

We know that the square function of the number four relates to the earth. On a three-dimensional level the square becomes a cube with width, length and height. It is the symbol of all earthly forms. In our physical form, we reflect the number four and the principle of the square and cube. In our spiritual essence, we relate to the number one and to the principle of the point and sphere. When we are in a harmonious relationship with God, we are like the point within the circle. Squaring the circle or circling the square is equivalent to fusing our earthly and spiritual essence. This was the sacred goal of all Mystery Schools.

A MASTER BUILDER IN YOUR OWN TEMPLE

Practice Is the First Step for the Student-Healer

Inner Space Awareness
Close your eyes. Gradually adjust to the silence within.

(5 minutes)

Mental Scanning
With your inner eyes (as if your eyes could see within), you will scan your insides. Your attention moves slowly from the top of your head to your toes...and slowly back to your head.... From one shoulder to the other... from one hip to the other...from front to back. (5 minutes, with eyes closed)

Does your inner space feel like a sphere? A cube? A combination of both? Can you mentally scan the space that feels like a sphere in a clockwise fashion?

Your mind continues to scan your insides. ...How does the space inside your limbs feel? Your arms...your legs?

Experience the relationship between the sphere within your head and the one within your chest, within your abdomen. Can you draw mentally an equilateral triangle from any one spot within your inner space (three equal sides)? One pointing upward, one pointing downward?

Can you visualize both triangles merging? (15 minutes)

Your Sanctuary
Your heart is a special place.
It is a place of rest.
A refuge in time of need.
Visualize the space inside your heart.
Feel it...sense it...
Examine the warmth inside your heart.
Feel it...sense it...
Examine the feeling that moves you right now.
Feel it...sense it…

Each thought is sacred as you are building your sanctuary with every thought that you have.

(5 minutes with closed eyes).

Through Law Love is Made Manifest

Inner cycles or laws that express the essence of reality determine all creation. When we digress from these laws, we lose the intrinsic harmony connecting all cycles of life with each other. Without fine-tuning we endanger the magic of our essential nature. What are these laws?

The first one is:

The Law of Unity

All is one and one is all. In this law we find the sacred meaning of Pythagorean' tetractys. It is the mystery of Unity in its relationship to multiplicity. The whole universe is reflected in a grain of sand. It is the mystery of the one God and its creation. It has been said that God is the circle whose center is everywhere and circumference nowhere. If we contemplate the point at the center of a sphere, the nature of our relationship with God is revealed. We are like a point within the sphere of God. When we are in harmony, we are right in the center of that point. To meditate on the point within the sphere is to expand in consciousness to the truth of our being.

Practice of the Law of Unity

Centering
Sit yourself comfortably.
Your thoughts quieten down...
Your breathing slows down...
Your attention goes to your heart.
Within the heart, visualize a light like the flame of a candle...
The light represents clarity.... Infinite love.... Infinite life...

Close your eyes
Look at the inner light. The light is growing bigger and bigger... it expands into a sphere. You are standing inside the sphere. You feel safe and secure within the sphere of light.

Join your hands in front of your heart.
Listen to the inner voice that says:
"I am in the center of the light."
Open your hands, palms out in a gesture of blessing.
"I share my inner clarity with the world at large."
The Law of Unity brings us to the next Law.

The Law of Opposites or Polarity

The spirit falls into matter and unity manifests itself in the world of form through multiplicity. Everything has two poles;

everything has its pair of opposites. Both aspects are identical in nature but different in degree. There are two sides to everything. If you draw a straight line from both sides of a point, two opposing directions are offered. For instance, you can either go to the right or to the left, or go up or down. Both paths emanate from the same point where opposites are reconciled. The horizontal line represents manifestation or creation on the material plane. The vertical line represents the descent of creative energy from a divine source. When a vertical line crosses at the point equidistant on the horizontal plane, you have the symbol of the cross. Although each religion focuses on a specific symbol, every symbol in its broader aspect has meaning for all. The Rosicrucians (Rose-Cross), an ancient secret society who claimed many humanists like Roger Bacon in their order, had for a symbol the rose at the center of the cross. The rose, symbol of beauty and purity, was seen growing at the junction of all four directions. The original meaning of the cross symbol devoid of its specific religious imprint, is the empowerment of the self through a new consciousness.

The horizontal axis represents humanity. It unifies heart and lungs with arms and hands. The point of connection between the horizontal and the vertical planes is where humanity stands. Will human beings stay at a crossroad, caught up in the struggle of opposites in the world of duality, or will they become the point of equilibrium and unite both poles? We have the choice. The straight line represents the Law of Opposites. Where two lines converge, a point is created with a potential for unity.

Shall we rise on a higher or downward spiral of consciousness? Our task is to develop consciousness of our potential.

EARTH AND HEAVEN INTERSECT AS A CROSS

Within Your Body Practice of the Law of Polarity

North South Direction. The vertical plane follows the spinal axis. Above the crown of your head imagine a light flowing down your throat, heart, solar plexus and abdomen all the way to your feet. It aligns the intellect and heart with the instinctive center. From the Heavens above, energy flows into the earth along this vertical line. From the ground up, earth energy moves along the same line. At the heart level, earth energy is tuned to that coming from the Heavens. At the point of the heart meditate on the merging of both energies. (5 minutes)

East-West Direction

The horizontal line follows the alignment of your arms in open expansion from your shoulders. When both arms and hands are on the same level on that plane, you create a horizontal line that passes through your heart center. This alignment demands an act of will since you cannot open your arms without sending a signal from your brain to your arms. Think about it! It represents the merging of your individual will with the essence of your heart. Close your eyes. Open your arms slowly, until you reach what you feel is the horizontal plane. This is your own will in motion. Your attention moves to your heart center as you slowly close your arms until your hands rest on your heart. Experience your heart energy merging with your individual will. (5 minutes)

The Cross

Both planes meet at your heart level. The cross of energy vibrates within you. When you become aware of the energy flow and feel it at your own level of understanding in your heart center, you become an alchemist with the power to transform universal energy at the level of your own heart. Think about it! The cross within your body is a symbol of energetic force more ancient than Christianity. It is a beautiful metaphor. The pole on the vertical plane symbolizes the masculine or electric force. It also symbolizes the energy from the Heavens above. The pole on the horizontal plane signifies the feminine or magnetic force. It also signifies the earth's energy. The point where both planes intersect becomes the center of a new life or union between earth and heaven activated by your own will. The center offers a solution to the problem of duality. The Two or opposites become one as it gives birth to the new.

The Law of Opposites or Polarity brings us to the next Law.

The Law of Gender

Everything has gender. Everything has a feminine and a masculine principle. Together they constitute a whole. Gender is in everything and manifests on all planes, mental, physical, emotional and spiritual. In the tiniest unit of matter there is a positive and a negative charge. Everything that becomes manifest comes as a result of the interplay between the positive and the negative or the masculine and feminine.

These are opposites not in terms of value judgment but in the nature of their charge. This power to beget or produce manifests in the animal and human organism as sex and it affects the smallest unit of matter through the negative and positive charge. This principle affects all planes. Within ourselves whether we are male or female, we have a masculine and a feminine side. To be aware of both sides is to maintain a perfect equilibrium.

On the mental plane, the positive phase is the conscious mind. The negative phase is the subconscious mind. When the two aspects connect and work together, this power to beget manifests as creativity. In the Chinese tradition, gender is seen as complementary. Yin the earth principle is feminine, passive, nurturing and yielding and Yang the male principle is active and assertive. Through their relationship all life becomes manifest in the Universe.

The right side of the body is associated with the active, masculine aspect of our personality, while the left side with the yielding, feminine aspect. At the level of the head there is a crossover, the right brain hemisphere relates to our intuitive faculties where the left hemisphere relates to our rational thinking. Both sexes share these two aspects. Our intuitive, yielding faculties grow out of our state of "being-ness". Our rational self is involved in "doing-ness". To be whole, both aspects need to co-exist in perfect harmony.

Practice of the Law of Gender

Silent Mind, Peaceful Body

The practice involves the achievement of an inner quiet mentally while being peaceful although alert physically. Both aspects co-exist at the same time. (You may be sitting or lying). With eyes closed allow the sense of tranquility to penetrate deep into the muscles of your feet. By and by, every muscle softens. Waves of tranquility roll gently, moving up toward your head.

Feel it.... Sense it.... Be Aware of it

A sense of peace is now flowing into your brain, soothing every nerve down your spine. Waves of peace infiltrate your whole nervous system.

Feel it.... Sense it.... Let it Be
A sense of joy sings its love tune into your heart. Its vibrations resonate along every vein, artery and capillaries.

Feel it.... Sense it.... Be it
Your mind is quiet...clear.... You feel yourself totally alive... totally aware of being right here, right now totally in tune, totally in charge.

Feel it.... Sense it.... Let it Be
The Law of Gender brings us to the next Law.

The Law of Vibration

"Nothing rests; everything moves; everything vibrates." The Kybalion.

Everything is energy in the Universe. Energy moves everywhere. Everything that is alive is in motion from the smallest cell to the largest galaxy. While everything vibrates, beings differ in their rate and mode of vibration. What we call matter and mind are different modes of vibratory motion. When we understand the law of vibration, we can raise our mental vibrations and mentally transmute the nature of our inner and outer environment. Every thought, every state has its corresponding rate and mode of vibration. Like attracts like. We can choose which kind of mental atmosphere we want in our life.

The Nature of Energy

Universal energy is everywhere. No function or activity can take place without energy. The Chinese call the Universal Life Force or energy Chi, the Japanese Qui. In Yoga practice, it is called prana or breath essence. In the Chinese medical tradition, vital energy flows throughout the body, along channels called meridians. Certain specific points along the spine, seven of them called chakras or wheels of force, act as focal energy points that relate to the four levels of our consciousness, mental, emotional, physical and spiritual.

Like notes on a scale, these centers resonate to a lower or higher pitch according to their position on the spine and to the individual's state of inner development. Each chakra corresponds to a glandular activity. These centers of consciousness are not physical in nature but are part of a subtler or psychic part of one's nature. They act as channels of subtle energies enabling one to discover a special attunement with the universal energy. The first three chakras relate to our lower nature and to the earth's energy. The first one is at the base of the spine, second below the navel, the third at the solar plexus. The last four are found in the upper part of the body, the heart, the throat, between the eyebrows and at the crown of the head. They relate to our higher level of consciousness.

If you think of yourself as a field of consciousness, before you can tune to a finer energy level and raise your frequency, you must clear every center or chakra to purify yourself.

Practice of the Law of Vibration

Clearing Chakras

When you consciously tune your attention to release what limits the flow in your system, you harmonize your field and increase your energetic potential.

Slowly draw the breath in through the nose and focus your attention on one chakra at a time, starting with the point between the eyes. When the outbreath follows, your attention is still and centered. Mental and emotional impurities will be released out of each chakra as you breathe out.

Starting on the point between the eyebrows, open your breath to peace and quiet.... As you breathe out, visualize the breath moving from your brow all the way up and out of the crown chakra. Same with each chakra, throat, heart, solar plexus, navel, all the way down to the root chakra.

Meditation on the Universal or Chi Energy

Standing up or sitting, imagine you are surrounded by Chi energy everywhere. From above your head, it flows like a shower of life all over you. Feel it on your face, your chest, and your back everywhere.... It flows through the crown of your head into your inner space. It expands to your fingers and toes. Every cell in your being is permeated by Chi energy. (Meditate on it for five minutes)

Tuning to a Higher Level
When you focus on an idea you individualize it which means you become a channel for the energetic transmission of this idea. Meditate on the Universal energy as it meets your heart chakra. Impress upon your heart a thought or a feeling that your heart desires. Hold it for a while. (Five minutes)

Energy Field
Close your eyes.... See yourself as an energy field. Once you have established yourself as an energy field...see yourself connecting with other energy fields.... All creation is energy.

The Law of Vibration brings us to the next Law.

The Law of Rhythm and Harmony

"The measure of the swing to the right, is the measure of the swing to the left; rhythm compensates." The Kybalion

Everything has Rhythm. The principle of rhythm arises from the principle of polarity. For every action there is a reaction. Rhythm manifests itself between two poles. All things rise and fall. All things have their cycles of peaks and valleys. Inner cycles, biological cycles, psychological rhythms, and seasonal cycles. Minerals, animals and plants have their own cycles. We evolve through rhythm when we merge with it rather than fight against it. To escape the influence of the pendulum swing on the lower plane, we learn to tune to a higher plane of consciousness. We rise to a higher spiritual plane when we become aware of the unifying quality of "prana" or life essence in the coming and going of the breath.

Practice of the Law of Rhythm and Harmony

Breath Meditation

Breath is life in motion. Your space is permeated with the essence of breath. When you center your breath in the silence of your heart, your body-space becomes sacred.

Pay attention to the breath right under your nostrils.

It flows down the nose's passage as slow as it wants to go…

And back…follow the breath further down the throat… and back… down the chest…and back.

It comes…and it goes…slowly and peacefully.

Wherever it wants to go…however long it wants to go, and back

Rolling in…rolling out.

The breath flows further down. To rest in your belly....

Feel your belly gently rise and fall. Slowly and peacefully.

Let the breath ride the crest of the wave...and back.

Your mind follows the breath...your mind is nestled in your breath. Close your eyes (5 minutes)

The Law of Rhythm and Harmony brings us to the next Law.

The Law of Cause and Effect

"Every Cause has its Effect. Every Effect has its Cause; everything happens according to Law."
—*The Kybalion.*

For everything one does or thinks, there will be a response. The human tendency is to attribute responsibility to external circumstances or to blame other people. All lives are intertwined yet we must accept responsibility, for the root of our experience lies within ourselves.

On our path of self-discovery, we must accept responsibility not only for our acts but for our thoughts as well. **"*Love thy neighbor as thyself*"** is a natural law of cause and effect. To do good to others is to receive in kind for good will comes right back to the source. This law is one of the most important for humanity to understand as it gives the key to our prosperity. This golden key was given to us more than two thousand years ago (Mark 12:31). When we feel excluded from love, health, money and self-esteem, somewhere within us we have excluded love, health, money and self-esteem. We cannot receive unless we learn to give. In aboriginal cultures, this law was very well understood as it was often the person who offered the gift who thanked the one who received it. The first person we have to give to is ourselves. Unless we have inner riches, we have nothing to give.

Practice of the Law of Cause and Effect

The Golden Key

To build our inner riches we make use of the golden key. To "golden key" a situation or a person, is to open the door to the flow of healing energy. It is a very simple and beautiful law that as a healer I use all the time.

To golden key someone or a situation requires:

1) In the silence of your mind, focus clearly on the person or situation that you want to golden key. (You might want to say to yourself, I golden key such and such.)

2) In the silence of your heart, concentrate on:

Unconditional love,
Infinite wisdom,
Infinite clarity,
Eternal peace,
Perfect harmony,
Absolute beauty,
Total joy. And let it go... You entrust it into the greater Mind, God.

The Law of Cause and Effect brings us to the next law.

The Law of the Triangle

The equilateral triangle with its three equal angles is the symbol of perfection. The first angle symbolizes the primal cause in its absolute perfection, the second the primal cause in manifestation and the third the product of the operation. As a sacred symbol, it expresses the divine principle of father and mother in the perfect relationship of creation to the child.

When one understands the meaning of the triangle, one has the key to regeneration and healing. The triangle conveys the idea that three forces are necessary for divine creation beyond and above the law of cause and effect that operates only on the material plane of duality. The law of the triangle is the key to mental power and absent healing. When it is well understood our prayers are very powerful.

Practice of the Law of the Triangle

Three Insights

On the mental plane, the power of prayers and healing operates by way of inner reflection over three aspects of a situation. These represent the three angles of the equilateral triangle where three makes one. To demonstrate and treat, our consciousness needs to acknowledge the following:

1. Primal cause: faith in divine perfection, the idea behind manifestation;

2. Cause in manifestation: the desire behind the idea or what you want to happen; and

3. Outcome of the operation: visualization of the idea.

Let's suppose that you want to treat for the health of a loved one:

1. Affirm that health is the expression of the One Mind's will.

2. Recognize in your own thoughts that (name the person) is expressing the will of the Absolute through a healthy life. To desire health, is to accept life wholeheartedly.

3. Visualize the person in good health...And let it go.

Entrust your treatment into the love of the One.... Thy will be done.

The Law of the Triangle brings the next Law.

The Law of Correspondence

"As above, so below" The Kybalion.

The law of correspondence is based on the principle of equilibrium. The lower level of the microcosm reflects the superior level of the macrocosm. The Seal of Solomon combines two interconnected triangles, one pointing up toward heavens, the other down toward the earth. It shows the perfect relation of the macrocosm and microcosm. The Seal of Solomon or Star of David is a symbol for all humanity for it illustrates the law of correspondence. The two triangles interlocked in our heart unlock the mystery of our divine spark. They expand our consciousness of our connection with the Divine.

The three points of the upper triangle represent:

1. The first aspect is First Cause: undifferentiated, containing everything and knowing nothing unlike itself.

2. The second is love: the individualized principle of First Cause. It reflects Oneness in its pure, perfect state.

3. The third is spirit turning into matter: the agent or divine spirit taking form.

The three points in the lower triangles represent:

1. The mind, self-consciousness and intellect

2. The soul, the individualized spark of divine spirit essence

3. The body, the physical manifestation.

The law of correspondence is used for practical demonstration in healing as it works from the belief to the manifestation. If we believe we shall have only a little good in our lives, we shall demonstrate only a little good. To the extent that we can enlarge our belief system, we shall enlarge our reality correspondingly.

Practice of the Law of Correspondence

A divine symbol, the Seal of Solomon is in your heart.

Imagine the base of one triangle as aligned with your solar plexus with the upper point pointing toward your throat. The base of the other triangle is at your heart level with the point toward your abdomen. Close your eyes. Meditate on the divine quality of the God in your heart which is at the center of the Seal of Solomon, "as above so below". In this instant you imbue yourself with the divine quality. Affirm in your heart that this divine quality will guide everything you do, say or act. (5 minutes)

The Law of Correspondence leads to the next Law.

The Law of the Octave

The completion of a cycle and the beginning of the new is based on the law of the octave. The chromatic scale in Western music is an octave. The eighth note of a music scale is either the last or first note of a scale. The seventh note is the one in which a modulation can take place to a lower or higher pitch. Based on the principle of the octave, a *new influx of energy* is needed before completing an old cycle and beginning a new one for the process to continue.

Cosmic creation culminates in the rest of the Seventh Day, for it can proceed no further until a fresh starting point is found. We start a new series in a Creative Octave when we become attuned with our Creator. The Resurrection takes place not on the Sabbath or Seventh day but on the Eighth Day which becomes the First Day of the new creative week. In this context, "Resurrection" can have a deep significance. Life after death is but a continuum on a higher scale.

Practice of the Law of the Octave

The Magic Wand

We focus on recognizing the end of a cycle and the beginning of a new one. All life proceeds through cycles whether in nature, people, or events. Within our life span we experience many cycles. When energy or interest is lacking in a situation, we are like a sail without wind. All we need is a strong breeze to get going. The magic wand is our ability to be aware of the divine spark within, our golden key, at the right moment. The insight offered by the law of the octave gives us a hint of the timing required.

Summary

The path leading to inner knowledge is the way of the healer. Knowing ourselves is to penetrate below the surface and experience the relationships between our mind, body, and spirit selves. To become whole is to be healed. To meditate on universal laws and principles helps us understand the interrelationship of all creation to the whole.

CHAPTER THREE

OUR SPIRITUAL ANATOMY

"The mind is one. Let man learn the revelation of all nature and all thoughts to his heart. The sources of nature are in his own mind, namely that the highest dwells within him."

¬Ralph Waldo Emerson,
The Essays of Ralph Waldo Emerson

I often tell my students that most people relate to their bodies the way an absentee owner relates to her or his income-producing estate. We delegate all responsibilities to anonymous employees, in this case our inner organs. It is about time that we take firsthand command of our affairs! The first principle before healing others is to heal ourselves. Healing starts at home! To that effect, we will look at our anatomy with fresh eyes. In this chapter, we will observe how our functioning relates to the universal laws we have just discovered and how to put their principles into practice.

What Does It Mean to Have a Spiritual Anatomy?

At the level of quantum physics, the stuff of the Universe is all energy[28]. Each person is a unique energy field, an open-ended system emitting and receiving energy. Processing energy all the time not only from what we eat and breathe but also from what we see, hear, think, feel and say, each one of us emits a unique vibration. Not being separate from the whole yet having our own center we are part of a wider energy field that encompasses the whole of life. In quantum terms, we are all connected. This view coincides with Dr. Carl C. Jung's notion of a collective unconscious[29] equivalent to a mental field. This field would consist of humanity's collective experience, including its archetypes. From a healer's perspective, Edgar Cayce shares the same view that the physical universe is a reflection of our consciousness[30]. At the highest level of our awareness, we know that we are grounded to the earth but spiritual in essence.

Seeing our physical organism from the view of our *threefold nature*, we observe that our head, chest and abdomen relate to different yet interrelated functions. Two areas interconnect our

---
28 The World within the World, p.169. John D. Barrow. Oxford University Press. 1988.
29 Psychology of the Unconscious. C.G.Jung. New York: Dodd, Mead. 1916.
30 The Edgar Cayce Handbook for Health through drugless Therapies. Dr. Harold J.Reilly and Ruth Hagy Brod. A Jove Book. 1977.

threefold nature: the throat with its thyroid gland and the solar plexus that regulates the sympathetic nervous system. For the healer, these two centers interconnect our thinking, feeling and instinctive activities, acting as entrance gates to regulate the constant flow of energy. When these two centers are balanced, our threefold nature is harmonized on an energetic level. We shall pay close attention to this process in our healing work.

The Thinking Function: The Head

Our Brain

We need to differentiate between brain and mind. Our brain, our mental equipment, with its two hemispheres or neocortex is the major component of our nervous system. In its physical context, it is a tool for thinking thoughts and retrieving memories. Our mind is our ability to think thoughts, create ideas and make use of our memory bank. At its highest level of awareness, when our mind reflects upon itself, it does so not only with the help of our mental equipment but through the whole of our conscious and unconscious activities. So that not only the brain but the spinal cord, the peripheral nerves and autonomic ganglia which comprise our central and autonomous nervous system may come into play. Doctor Paul MacLean, a chief of the Laboratory of Brain Evolution and Behavior of the National Institute of Mental Health, discovered the functions of three separate brains that regulate our central and autonomous nervous system that he called the triune brain[31].

Our Triune Brain

This model altogether comprises the Rhesus complex, the limbic brain and the neocortex. The first brain, the Rhesus complex or reptilian brain is shared in common with all animals. It is the most ancient brain that involves body movements, sensory impressions, and survival of self. The second brain or limbic brain we share with all mammals. It controls relationships, emotions, the immune system, biorhythms, and self-healing. The third brain or neocortex regulates the activities of abstract thinking, our will, and all human creativity. This is the new brain in our evolution, a privilege shared by all humanity.

The complexity and wealth of this vast neurological organism constitute "who and what" we are. Our next challenge is to bring these unfolding processes to our conscious awareness and by doing so reach another plateau of development.

Our Mind

Ernest Holmes, one of the finest metaphysical teachers and pioneers of the New Thought movement, describes our awakening in this way:

---

[31] The Dragons of Eden. Carl Sagan. Random House, N.Y. 1977.

"The first great discovery man made was that he could think. This was the day when he first said "I am". This marked his first day of personal attainment. From that day man became an individual and had to make all further progress himself. From that day there was no compulsory evolution; he had to work in conscious union with life. He had perceived that Nature works through him rather than works for him."[32]

The tool of our mental creativity is the mind. How else could we reflect, ponder, imagine, memorize, and meditate? Our thoughts, product of our mind, can go in all directions or be in active or reflective modes. But who does the thinking? Zen Buddhists make us ponder this when they recognize a small mind and a big mind, although they see it as one mind.

What they call small mind is our human mind. Our birthright is to develop our intellect, but on our own we might get limited by our prejudices, opinions, limited experiences, and cultural milieu. The result is a personality overrun by the ego. But what of big mind? It is the mind which is not related to anything outside self (e.g., opinions and prejudices) and therefore without any dualistic tendencies or fragmentation of self. We are told "big mind is that which contains everything within itself" including small mind! Small mind within big mind may be perceived as Universal Mind or God. One is within the other[33]. Ernest Holmes conceives the Universality of Mind shared by

---

32   Open At The Top. The Life of Ernest Holmes. Neal Vahle Open View Press, Mill Valley Calif. 1993. Appendix p.141.
33   Zen Mind. Beginner's Mind. Shunryu Suzuki. Weatherhill,Inc., N.Y. 1970.

all thinkers as one power, one system of universal operations, one operating intelligence for the whole cosmos.

Our Immune System

The key to our health maintenance is our immune system. When the immune function does not work, either by doing too little or too much, there is exposure to offensive substances. Major glands like the hypothalamus and the thymus, one in the center of the head and the other right above the heart, play a major role in this regulation. The hypothalamus is situated in the middle brain of what MacLean calls the "neural chassis". The neural chassis contains both the Rhesus complex and the limbic system so that sensory impressions and our sense of survival interface with emotions, biorhythms and self-healing. This chamber-like cavity also acts as a spiritual center in receiving and distributing the Chi energy, the stuff of all activity and life in the universe.

In the middle brain with a special connection to the hypothalamus is found the pineal gland, a gland unexplained in medical terms but believed to be a receiver of cosmic energy. By way of the thalamus spread on both sides of its chamber, the hypothalamus regulates the activity of the pituitary gland in charge of a vast range of hormonal controls and acts as a distributor of Chi energy.

Edgar Cayce, a well-respected healer and author of many books on healing, notes the importance of the ductless gland pituitary[34]. "That which connects the pineal to the pituitary may be truly called the silver cord which is the creative essence in physical, mental and spiritual life; for the destruction wholly of either will make for the disintegration of the soul from its house of clay."

The Stress Response

The nervous system and the adrenal glands are linked in several ways. In response to stress messages from the brain, the adrenal glands release hormones into the blood and mobilize the body's energy reserves. When we over-react out of fear or pain, we deplete our energy bank. We call this the fight or flight response. The adrenals should only provide emergency energy.

When too many "stress hormones" are released, the production of antibodies and white cells are inhibited and the immune system is lowered. Among white cells are the natural "killer" cells called T-lymphocytes and macrophages responsible for fighting against infection and other diseases. If stress is the off switch that depresses our system's ability to fight disease, peace and harmony are the on switch that restores its innate potential.

---

[34] The Edgar Cayce, Handbook for Health through drugless Therapy. Dr. Harold J. Reilly. A Jove Book 1977.

The placebo effect demonstrates the use of the mind in healing. The repair process goes on all the time and we have a role to play in going deeper into the body's inner intelligence with our creative mind. Thoughts create biochemical reactions in our tissues. Whenever a thought flares up, it triggers a chemical response called a neurotransmitter. We can train our mind to internalize new conditions that will positively affect our organism.

The Bridge between the Thinking and Feeling Functions: The Throat

The throat is the area of transition between the thinking and feeling functions. The throat or fifth chakra is the first of the last three chakras or wheels of energy that relates to our higher sense of consciousness as described in Chapter Two. The throat center may resonate to a higher pitch. It vibrates to the number five that represents the newly born spirit in human beings. It is the door of the higher centers where thoughts and feelings merge and where our voice originates. The throat represents a new challenge in our development.

The fifth chakra corresponds to the thyroid, a ductless gland with internal secretions that escape directly into the lymph stream and the blood vessels. Situated at the front and sides of the throat, the thyroid secretes hormones needed for growth and maintenance of our metabolism. The thyroid is controlled by the pituitary gland in the head and influences the thymus gland located right above the heart. We will remember that number five represents the pentagon or the five-pointed star blessing the coming of the new child. We may visualize the thyroid gland radiating its loving secretions above the chamber of our heart. When our thoughts express the feelings in our heart, we own our voice for the first time and we express our true nature.

The Feeling Function: The Chest

The chest, our feeling center, is positioned midway between our mental and instinctive centers. Housing the heart and lungs, it serves as a transmission station for both blood and breath's circulation.

The Heart

The heart is the central organ of our whole being forming a functional whole with the circulatory system of the blood and the breathing function. Rudolf Steiner points out that the blood circulation with the arteries, veins and capillaries belongs to the metabolic pole opposed to the nerve sense system.

"The heart is the place where these two polarities meet bringing equilibrium and harmony." [35]

---
35 Spiritual Science and the Art of Healing. Rudolf Steiner's Anthroposophical Medicine. Victor Bott, M.D. Healing Arts Press, 1984. Translated and republished 2004 by Rudolph Steiner Press.

The circulation of the venous blood into the heart goes through a rhythmic phase of diastole which is a centrifugal process of dilatation followed by a systole phase which is a centripetal nerve-sense reaction of contraction. Diastole and systole are then the expression of two polarities. The heart maintains the equilibrium of this rhythmic system by being the chamber where these two opposites come into harmony. The heart is meant to be healthy and is usually the last organ in our system to give up.

Right above the heart where we find the fourth chakra, the thymus gland hovers like a guardian angel to protect our metabolism. With its direct connection to the spleen and the lymphatic system it helps maintain the right production of T-lymphocytes and antibodies to reinforce our immune system.

The Lungs

Lungs are the organs that start to function when we are born as terrestrial beings. They are instrumental in the incarnation of our soul. With the first inspiration, our lungs connect us to the outside physical world, while with the last expiration our life-time connection is severed. The constant dual rhythmic process of breath or vital life essence pulses by way of our lungs through our circulatory system. It establishes a unique connection to our environment as well as our inner world. Breath has a unique quality of renewing the vitality of our blood which in turn has an important role in the exchange of substances in the tissues with its warmth and mobility. The lung is strongly connected to the nervous system. With simple observation of the breath rhythm, we acquire the ability to deepen our breathing function with a calming effect on our nervous system.

The Bridge Between the Feeling and the Instinctive Functions: The Solar Plexus

The solar plexus or third chakra acts as a subtle transition between the *feeling* and the *instinctive* function. In medieval times, the solar plexus that is part of the autonomous nervous system was called the small brain since it records and internalizes our emotions. One of three gangliated plexuses to form the sympathetic nervous system, the solar plexus is situated in front of the middle spine. It extends its plexus of nerves and fibers to the back of the stomach sending information to the network connecting thoracic and pelvic cavities

Too often information is unconsciously recorded in our nervous system and mounting stress pushes the buttons of the adrenal glands triggering a *fight or flight response*. When decoded by our finer sentiments with the help of self-awareness and the practice of meditation, this raw emotional energy can be transformed into healing energy. When that happens, the solar plexus becomes a transformer blending and fusing lower abdominal energy into that of the heart center. Both throat and solar plexus transmute energy from one area to the other.

The Instinctive Function: The Abdomen

The abdominal cavity is the center of our instinctive activities. In Ancient Temples, the purgatorial chambers of initiation were always subterranean, representing the windings of intestinal tracts. The central nervous system or cerebrospinal connects to the sympathetic system relating our sense impressions to the brain. According to the Ancient Brahmin Tradition, the tube Shushuma in the center of the spine reflects on a subtle level the macrocosm through the seven flowers of the chakra plexuses.

Two cords or pneumogastric nerves converge from the medulla oblongata or Rhesus complex which stores and determines instinctive behavior, down the left and right of the spine to the pelvic cavity forming a single ganglion in front of the first chakra or root chakra. Also referred to as the vagus nerves from the Latin to meander, well known in the oldest Vedic texts in Hinduism by their Sanskrit names Ida and Pingala, their function on the etheric or subtle level is the transformation of unconscious into conscious activities.

Mrs. Helena Blavatsky, who in 1875 founded the Theosophical Society in New York City (theosophy means "Divine Wisdom"), mentions in one of her books the "Secret Doctrine" that the Shushuma is keyed to the musical note A and that the Ida and the Pingala are the sharp and flat of this central tone influenced by the activity of the nostrils on their respective sides. The Ida is like the Moon and the Pingala like the Sun. From the most primitive center in the brain to the coccyx at the base of the spine the two sympathetic cords are awaiting their awakening to higher consciousness.

On an energy level, our feeling center as a whole can be affected by both mental and instinctive centers according to the level of development of the fifth chakra or solar plexus and third chakra or throat center, both acting as threshold of passage of Chi energy.

Let's continue the road leading to the mystery of our nature. We experience living on four levels: physical, mental, emotional and spiritual. Physical contains all. Mental accesses all. Emotional disturbs or quiets all. Spiritual heals all.

Physical Contains All

When imbalance sets on any of these levels, a disruption of energy follows disturbing the potential for wholeness. The practice of self-awareness keeps our energy level in balance and develops our ability to focus attention. Attention is the key to fusing our threefold nature.

Mental Accesses All

When the mind is tuned to the heart, it possesses the healing power. Scientists say that the brain sends neuro-transmitters to every part of the body. Every time the brain emits a conscious signal, an electro/chemical component appears at the site. Which means right where the thought leads! What an enormous responsibility to think the right thought! And what is the right thought? Isn't it the one that is in tune with our heart? By means of meditation and breathing awareness the mind is calmed and the body responds in kind. Our attention, function of the mind based on inner quiet, will direct the flow of our thoughts.

Emotional Disturbs or Quietens All

In the tranquility of our inner being, we discover our inner feelings, our emotions. We need to weed out in the quiet of our heart what we know to be love-lessness. Negative emotions poison our system. To heal we need to surrender the emotional life-denying pattern that stresses each organ. While mental memory is selective, the body remembers the emotional content of a painful experience. It is imprinted in the cellular memory while the conscious mind is actively blocking it out. It stays in the memory bank waiting to be released. The release of the free flow of vital energy has to happen through the body!

Spiritual Heals All

Spiritual is our finer level of being. It is the plane of creativity where imagination, intuition and finer sentiments operate. Through meditation and affirmation, we access all levels of our nature in harmony with the One power where all creation comes from, at last realizing that we are also spiritual beings and that the more conscious we are, the more our divine nature is expressed in our livingness. Let's introduce some practices in our daily lives to nurture the person we really are.

The goal of healing is to fuse primal energy with the higher energy centers in the head and heart, restoring the balance yearned by the whole system. As we use and practice conscious attention and awareness we have the ability to re-pattern our entire nervous system.

Practice

1. Meditation

2. To be present right here and now

3. Mental awareness of the location of each organ within your body

4. The transmutation of negative into positive consciousness

5. The power of creative awareness and affirmation

Meditation

Sit comfortably with your back and head straight.

Feel the ground under your feet.

Cup your right hand into your left and place both hands on your lap.

Take a moment to adjust your awareness to your sitting position.

Close your eyes.

Feel the silence within.

Let all tension dissolve.

Your attention is focused on the breath coming in and out of your nose.

Slow down your breath.

Invite the breath to flow all the way to your cupped hands and back to your nose.

(5 minutes)

Being Present Here and Now

The practice of attention is the basis of the law "like attracts like." The healer's responsibility is to make a choice. Our thoughts change the quality of our life. Whenever we practice self-awareness, we are actually practicing Yoga in its innermost essence. We practice attention by:

Observing

How do I feel right now? Can I focus attention on my face...chest...abdomen? Close your eyes. Stay within your own inner silence for a while. Enter your own space. Your attention moves with your breathing gently flowing in and out... (5 minutes)

Do it several times during the day.

Sensing

Can I sense the skin around my face...my chest... abdomen...back? What about the air around me? The ground under my feet? Close your eyes and practice sensing. (5 minutes).

Do it several times a day.

Locating Each Organ in the Body

Can I locate mentally the organs within my body? In which part of my anatomy is my liver located? Do I know where my pancreas lies? My kidneys? Where is my stomach located?

Your stomach is centrally located below your rib cage. Place your hand where your stomach is. Move your hand to the right where your liver lies. The gallbladder is right behind it. To the left of your stomach and slightly behind it, lies your pancreas and further to the left is your spleen. On each side of the spine, below your shoulder blades hang your adrenal glands, one to the right and one to the left. Right below the adrenals stand your kidneys. One to the right, the other to the left. Your intestinal tract starts below your stomach. Behind lies the bladder and a female or male reproductive system.

(Close your eyes. Try to locate all organs mentally. 5 minutes)

Body Scanning

Sit comfortably and close your eyes. Take a couple of minutes to get used to the silence within. Sense your breathing come and go peacefully. You can see with your mind's eyes the open space within your head. Your eyes have become like two light beams functioning as a scanner. Mentally list what you see and feel: eyeballs, inner ear, the conduit of your nose, mouth, throat and so on.

You are now scanning further down your chest, observing leisurely the inner area that includes your lungs and heart. Stay there for a little while...then continue further down toward your stomach and look at the lining inside the stomach. Take your time. Behind the stomach on both sides of the spine look at the kidneys. And right on top of them look at the two small glands, the adrenals. Can you feel your breathing come and go in that area...You are almost halfway through scanning and you are doing very well, so don't give up!

To the right of the stomach, your inquisitive eyes will look at the liver and right behind it the gallbladder. Feel your breathing come and go in this area... explore the inside of the liver... As you are scanning to the left, look at the pancreas and the spleen. Invite your breathing, like a gentle breeze to come and go to that side... Now take a plunge toward the abdomen and discover the meanders of the intestinal tract, large and small intestine. Send the breath to navigate back and forth toward the abdomen... Further down, your eyes are scanning the bladder, the ovaries and uterus for women and prostate and seminal vesicles for men. Bravo, you have done it!

Transmuting Negative into Positive

To help dissolve the negative imprint of the "cellular memory" of a specific organ, based on our understanding of the principle of polarity, we apply the law of *correspondence*.

Polarity

A helpful model shows that each organ is vulnerable to a specific negative emotion and is influenced by its corresponding positive counterpart. For example:

Our *liver* and *gallbladder* are affected by anger, fear, frustration and guilt. The opposite emotions are clarity, peace, harmony and a sense of fun.

Our *stomach* is affected by fear of the unknown, and a sense of powerlessness. The opposite is our trust in life, and the ability of letting go into the greater power in whom we live and have our being.

Our *pancreas* is affected by a sense of affective loss, the sweetness gone out of life. The opposite is loving care, being able to accept the love of others and caring for ourselves.

Our *spleen* is affected by a sense of unfinished business relating to loved ones, by heaviness in the heart. Every time the child in you had a broken heart, the energetic field in the spleen got diminished. The opposite is the amazing healing power of forgiveness together with a heightened awareness of the loving potential in everyone.

Our *kidneys* are affected by impure thoughts, by mental confusion. Every time you avoid seeing the truth, you poison yourself. The opposite is clarity of mind. The ability to see your own truth.

Our *adrenals* are affected by anxiety, a lack of trust, a sense of limitation, and a lack of faith. The opposites are peace and harmony.

Our *reproductive glands* are affected by unconscious guilt, confusion and prejudice. The opposites are appreciation of life on its own natural terms, recognizing beauty in all its manifestations and giving thanks for the blessings of life.

Our *heart* is affected by stress, fear of loneliness and death. The opposites are inner peace and the awareness of our essential nature. We are never alone when we realize our true divine nature.

Our *lungs* are affected by a sense of limitation and a lack of joy. The opposite is self-motivation, moving forward in mind with creative ideas, and cultivating a joyful appreciation for life. Our *throat* is affected by low self-esteem, fear of being exposed, and self-denial. The opposite is realizing one's true nature. When you recognize your own divine nature, you find your own individual sound and the ability to express it.

Our *brain* is affected by unconscious fear, busy thoughts that never let go. The opposites are the silence and tranquility achieved with the practice of meditation.

What we do not want to see and what we do not want to hear affect our eyes and ears. The opposites are mental openness and ability to go within looking for truth.

Correspondence

Correspondence based on the principle of polarity is the cornerstone of healing. It is the bridge that joins the idea to its manifestation. How do we make use of the law of correspondence? When we substitute in mind the negative for the life-giving quality of a specific organ.

Matching Each Organ to Its Corresponding Emotion and Polarity or Opposite

Sit yourself comfortably and close your eyes.

Your breathing settles within your own silence. After a while, have your eyes scan your "inner" landscape and go mentally to your liver and gallbladder area. Mentally name the emotion that might have stressed these organs. In order to release all negative energy, it might be helpful to imagine a tiny pump right inside each organ with the ability to suck all negative emotions out. With your mind's eyes, see all the stale energy released. Let it go.... Now comes the change. Visualize a golden light and its infinite power of good, restoring life energy in the liver and gallbladder. Every cell in your liver and gallbladder is infused with this quality. The golden light takes the quality of the corresponding positive emotion... Hold on to the thought as long as it feels comfortable...

(Same process applies for each organ.)

Start with the abdominal area.

Place your hand where your liver is...Close your eyes.

Feel your breath gently flowing in and out toward your hand.

"I now give every cell in my liver permission to release...*anger*...*fear*.

In its place every cell in my liver is now fully alive breathing *joy and happiness*"

Slowly open your eyes

Repeat the same process "transmute negative into positive" with each organ in the abdominal area. After clearing these organs, proceed to the head center and finish with the chest center. With every organ repeat the same procedure as needed. It is up to you to find the positive equivalent of the negative. Use your own creativity. You will find it is a very powerful process.

Make sure to give thanks in your heart. This is the way to entrust the whole process into the hands of the bigger power, the big Mind!

Tuning to a Higher Consciousness through Prayer and Affirmation

The Power of Prayer and Affirmation

What are they? Prayer and Affirmation are ways we communicate with the transcendental power in which we live and have our being. We call it infinite Intelligence or infinite Love. World religions and healers through the ages have provided vital guidance and have contributed their knowledge to humanity. It is inherent in every human being and transcends specific religious practice. Love is the common denominator of all forms of prayers. Too often, in our ignorance, we limit the practice to times of imminent danger and mostly in the asking mode. Would we converse with a loved one only in time of need? The power of prayer is in the quality of the thought and the intent behind it.

It might be done in a *direct* mode with a clearly defined intent like a request or the *indirect*, open-ended mode of union with infinite Intelligence. Both modes are appropriate at different times. In any case a sense of surrender, the small mind merging with the big mind, "*Thy will be done*", is the ground for union and healing.

It is an impulse from the heart. It can be a:

State of union,
Evocation,
Invocation,
Affirmation, or
Confirmation.

Its power is in its attunement to a higher level of consciousness. Our inner spark merges in union with the infinite power of Life. The state of oneness reaches through time and space. Our *healing affirmation* or *visualization* heals through distance and is called absent healing.

PRACTICE

Healing Affirmation

When we do a healing treatment, it is important to address it in the present and in the affirmative mode.

For example:

I am (if it is for yourself or name the person for whom is the treatment) in a state of perfect harmony mentally, spiritually and physically. Perfect order is in my (his/ her) life.

Each one of the millions of cells in my (or name) organism is responding to divine light, love and life. Each cell is in perfect living order right now. And so, it is!

And let it go.... To the higher power...!

Give thanks in your heart for the healing and surrender yourself to the Higher power. It does the work, not you.

Another Healing Affirmation

Deep within (me or name the person),

Where once there was fear, there is now trust.

Where once there was anger, there is now tolerance.

Where once there was hate, there is now unconditional love.

A most beautiful prayer is the prayer of Saint Francis of Assisi, the gentle Italian monk who in the 13th century dedicated his life as a prayer to God. He saw all creation, be it the sun, the moon, the stars or the animals, as his brothers and sisters in God. He left us a simple prayer that beautifully illustrates his vision for the release of negative emotions.

Prayer of Saint Francis

Lord, make me an instrument of your peace!
Where there is hatred...let me sow love.
Where there is injury.... pardon.
Where there is discord...unity.
Where there is doubt...faith.
Where there is error...truth.
Where there is despair.... hope.
Where there is darkness...light.
Where there is sadness...joy.
O Lord, grant that I not so much desire
to be consoled, as to console,
to be understood, as to understand,
to be loved, as to love,
For it is in giving, that we receive,
It is in pardoning, that we are pardoned,
It is in dying, that we are born to eternal life.

Summary

We gain invaluable insights when we realize we are all energy, part of the Cosmos in essence. With wonder we discover that our body has its own intelligence. Within our head, chest and abdomen are centers corresponding to specific functions. These centers interconnect through a network of glands and nerve tissues. Developing inner awareness becomes the foundation of our healing power. We achieve harmony as we practice meditation and relaxation on a daily basis. It has a direct effect on the health of our immune system bringing equilibrium to both endocrine and autonomous nervous systems. It supplies the adrenals with unlimited resources of comfort so they do not fire into activity before real need. We discover with wonder the tremendous skills displayed by our organism. Its intelligence needs our recognition so that we can engage in a creative partnership. Every time we nurture positive thoughts, our body reacts positively. Our healing potential is a function of our heart's development.

CHAPTER FOUR

HEALING

"You are a beacon of light."

—Ethel Lombardi

Healing Demands A Radical Change of Attitude

Plato once said that human beings live as if in a dark cave not knowing that the light of day is shining outside. When we accept the visible world as the only reality, we emulate the cave dwellers. We can change by awakening our consciousness. In the Bible we have a beautiful metaphor: Eve eats from the Tree of Knowledge and immediately knows that she is naked. If enough people practice a new way of seeing, a new reality will emerge. In the evolution of our culture, every time a new perception is awakened, a change takes place. When Europeans realized that the sun was the true center of our planetary system rather than the earth, they reached the Americas.

By the same token, when we discover our spiritual sun, our position within our own universe tilts. No longer are we centered on our small ego. We dare challenge preconceived opinions and discover our nakedness, our essential self. Our guiding spirit provides our new clothes. The merging of our small ego with our guiding spirit is a source of tremendous strength. It is the basis of healing dynamics.

In the summer of 1996, I was conducting a healing program for cancer patients of the Lombardi Center at the Georgetown Hospital in Washington DC. One of the patients in my group named Bonnie asked if I could be present during her surgery. Bonnie was to undergo a radical mastectomy on both sides followed by reconstruction. I welcomed her invitation and, after receiving the surgeon's permission to assist her in the O.R., I gave her healing sessions over a two-week period to help her prepare for surgery.

During five hours of surgery, I sat behind Bonnie with hands over her head. I initially sensed great perturbation. I could feel the intensity of the turmoil inside her brain as she was being prepared for surgery. Each side of her cortex vibrated at a different ratio. Within twenty minutes both sides had calmed down. At that very moment, the anesthetist was surprised to see an even pattern on his screen. An indication that the patient needed less anesthesia!

I was the first smiling face that Bonnie saw when she woke up in the operating room. By all accounts from the medical team, the five-hour surgery had been a complete success. A nurse noted the unusual atmosphere that prevailed in the O.R. She confided with a giggle that "everybody was on their best behavior!" Fancy having a healer around! An atmosphere of great peace and concentrated attention replaced the usual tone of banter and jokes that usually occurs, no doubt to relieve the extreme tension of a medical team during long hours of focused attention. Bonnie's recovery was unusually prompt. Three years later she was still in perfect health.

A New Attitude Toward Death and Dying

Life's paradox is that although our physical existence is bound to the earth, we are transient beings on our beautiful planet. Like breath that expands and contracts allowing for rest in between, there is another side to physical life. Observing cycles of growth and decay in nature, we see death and dying as the other part of that rhythm. A culture with too much emphasis on material goods places a greater premium on the life of the body than the life of the soul. This does not help us to face our fear of death and dying. When we discover what we really are, a spirit ensouled in a body, we awaken to the possibility of being multidimensional. This eases the fear of separateness or death.

Healing and Traditional Medicine

The healing practitioner does not deny traditional medicine. Healing therapy does not pretend to be a cure-all and works best as preventive medicine. A positive mental attitude speeds up the process of change and affects our inner chemistry. It is effective in supporting the recovery process as it enhances wholeness. Based on the intimate relationship between state of mind and body functions, it provides the immune system with a therapeutic booster. It offers a realistic way to take charge and maintain one's health at a maximum level.

The Practitioner

We are all potential healers. We can heal ourselves and we can heal others. The healing practitioner sees him or herself as a channel. It is not his or her energy that is at stake but the unending source available through our connection with the infinite Power. The healer becomes a conduit, a guide to a safe awakening of new possibilities and the integration of one's holistic nature. Mental and spiritual awareness are channeled through the body. Whatever needs to be released is *released through the body!*

I often compare the body to the final production of a play. What one sees on stage is the final result. Before the performing comes the idea, the writing, the acting, the setting and the staging. Without all these elements, no performance could take place. Where it is all revealed is in the final product. One does not see what happens behind the scene. Change one element, it will show in the play on stage. Same with the body.

Healing as a Personal Experience

We behold the mystery of our spiritual nature. Although our body is secondary to the spirit, it is part and parcel of it. We need to consider our anatomy as sacred as we are in reality a spirit ensouled in a body. How would organs know how to cooperate with each other if cells did not have their own consciousness? With a little bit of imagination, we can see ourselves function like a hologram traveling through time and space as we partake of life's creation in a very physical capsule! Never denying our very earthy nature, we may one day retrieve the inner vision of the starry space.

Before you can go into the practice of Healing, you have to make yours the principles developed in the previous part of this book. Each individual who is clear and willing can entrust his or her higher self to know when one is ready. But before that happens, one has to be willing to work at it.

A healer holds the vision of a field within fields, body, mind and spirit and sees her/his field of energy expand as a channel of a universal energy force, not just of her/his own limited energy. Our responsibility is to maintain our own field as clear as possible. Of these three fields, the body is the densest. It is where all other functions make their imprint. Although the densest, the body has its own intelligence. It remembers everything and can help the mental level to retrieve emotional information often lost under pressure caused by denial or pain!

What is a Field? For a healer a field is the energy that emanates from the state of being just as we are. Our physical state reflects an "aura" of light also called the etheric field that may be perceived by trained eyes. We share in common with plants the potentialities of the etheric field. Our emotional state is imprinted on an astral field which also surrounds us and which we have in common with animals. Negative emotions imprinted on the astral field, block the vital flow of energy that needs to circulate along the body.

When there is confusion in the astral field, a result of our emotional state, it affects the etheric sheath, which in turn reflects our state of general health. Higher vibrational frequencies of spiritual consciousness are recorded on a much subtler field that is multidimensional and acts as a support system to our physical sheath as it affects for the best both the etheric and the astral.

The Energy Field is Sensitive to Mental Energy

Our ability to think or "small mind" creates all the time. Its tool is our brain that has the task to search, clear, tune, harmonize.

Our cells have their own consciousness. Their vibratory state is imprinted on our etheric sheath or aura and it responds to mental energy. Through the brain, our mental activity accesses the body and reflects the soul. We are pioneers in a new field of communication. Our goal is to transmit signals at the cellular level.

Mind is Power Energy

The mind is the door to healing. When we use the power of our mind, our mental energy, we have access to a new reality that reaches out everywhere our mind can conceive. Ernest Holmes, the founder of the Science of Mind philosophy, says that within us is the power of the spirit backed up by our mental energy. It is our consciousness in operation.

Prayer or affirmation is the Highest Form of Power Energy

Some people have claimed that God is dead, for if God existed this and that would not happen. Indeed, the bounty of the Universe will not force itself upon us. We have arrived at a time in the evolution of humankind where the microcosm has to be conscious of the macrocosm where its origin lies. The journey back home is an act of self will. We have the tools of our intellect and the freedom of choice to align ourselves with the unlimited power of unconditional Love. Love is God's vibration. We have to be "self-starters" for the alignment to operate. There is no individual God to pull us up by our own bootstraps. The miraculous power of aligning our mind to the higher energy of unconditional Love is what we call prayer.

Clear Negative Emotions

Each organ relates to an energy field. This energy or etheric field has the original cellular memory. When an organ is missing the field is still there. We always treat the field not the organ itself. When there is dis-ease, the original blueprint has been disturbed. Emotional reactions affect the cellular memory of the nervous and glandular systems.

Our Tools:

Our hands, a channel of our mental, spiritual and physical being, are our healing tools together with visualization of the spirit in action.

But also:

Our heart as love, tolerance and hope.
Our lungs as vital breath, God's invisible pulse.
Our feet as our ground and connection to mother earth.
Our arms as action, mobility, choice and independence.
Our eyes as the windows of our soul.

Hands

In loving interaction our hands provide a message of wellbeing and care. Their wonderful quality is to communicate warmth. As a healing practitioner of many years, my hands are fine antennae into the world of others. Inside the palm of each hand, a wheel of force or chakra awaits to be awakened. Both right and left hands receive and emit energy. The left hand has the added quality of pulling blocked energy out of the way. The guideline for hands placement during a healing session is based on the understanding of our threefold nature.

Major hands placement:

1. *on or above the chest as* our feeling center

2. *on or above the head as* our thinking center

3. *on or above our abdomen as* our instinctive center

With two major thresholds

4. *our throat* holds deep emotions

5. *our solar plexus as the* center of our nervous system

Position of the Hands

During a healing session, both hands are always positioned on, over or around a center. A center is a focal point. It can be a particular organ or gland; a chakra located in the chest, head or abdominal area; as well as the throat or solar plexus.

The following is a list of the most basic hand positions.

Standard: one hand flat positioned on, over, under or above a center.

Double Standard: both hands positioned on, over, under or above a center.

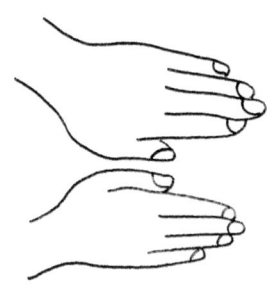

Straight Line: fingers touching as both hands form a straight line from that point. Both hands can be on the body or above.

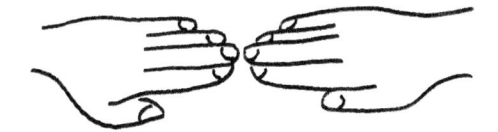

Angle Position: one hand lies on a straight line while the other adjusts its position to the center with the angle needed.

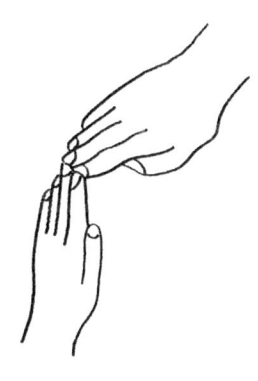

V Position: From a center point a V is created by both hands with fingers going upward to form an open angle.

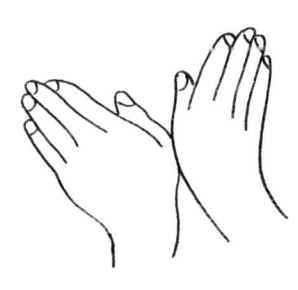

A Position: Toward a center point an A is created with fingers joining together to form a small angle with both hands outstretched.

Star Position: A star is built from a center with the use of three positions, a V and A and a straight line.

Cradle Position: with fingers interlocking, both hands create like a cradle that is used mainly to surround the throat or the jaw area.

Practices offered in previous chapters are like multidimensional road maps in preparing us for:

Hands on Healing

Above all the heart center needs to be open!

Review your guidelines:

Attitude
You are a multi-dimensional field of energy. As an atomic structure, you emit and receive energy. As a spiritual healer you are tuned to the frequency of your heart chakra.

Position in Space
Whether standing, sitting or lying down, feel grounded. What does it mean? It means to be aware "here and now" of your position in space and of your contact with the ground. If you are standing, pay attention to the ground under your feet. Allow your full weight as well as your breathing to flow into your feet. If you are sitting down, become aware of the chair under your seat as well as the ground. Same if you lie down.

Centering
What does it mean? It means to be present within yourself. You achieve the sense of inner presence by paying attention to your breathing.

Breathing Awareness

Breathing awareness is Chi energy. Allow your breath or Chi the freedom to be. Remember that breath is the invisible pulse of life.

Mental Clarity

Leave your busy thoughts outside the door. Let go of them by taking a deep breath, and clear yourself of any fear, doubt and anxiety. Your mental mode is set on openness and attention.

Spiritual Focus

Center your attention on your heart. The little flame in your heart grows into a glowing sun where love, life and light vibrate. Feel the glow emanating and expanding to reach your patient. Every time you need reassurance, go right back into your heart

HANDS-ON HEALING

Hands-on healing is a fulfilling experience. It takes place as your hands stand above or on your client's body from the subtlest to the densest, from the inner to the outer field of energy.

Keep a clear and alert mind. Let go of any fear or confusion if it comes. Keep your focus alert, clear your mind and tune into your inner spark. A quick clearing and affirmation will prevent you from processing your own issues. This is not what you are here to do. If at times your mind wanders and you find yourself distracted, quickly go into your "golden key" or focus on the divine spark in your heart. Have no *expectations* of what may happen. Trust the guiding hand of your intuition, your angel of light. At the beginning you might wonder how long you should leave your hands in one place. Each position might demand from a couple of minutes to twenty depending on the situation. From time to time you will be given a time frame. As a rule, stay long enough to develop your own sense of what is going on. The whole session might take an hour or less and will be welcome by your patient!

The Opening

Offer the recipient time to sit or lie down while you wash your hands. (Your hands should be washed before and after the session.) Have the person lie flat on her or his back. Make sure they are comfortable by placing one or two pillows under their knees. Also cover their body with a light blanket so they will feel warm and cozy. Place yourself standing or sitting behind the recipient. The opening of a session is meant as a short introduction so people can become acquainted before the actual sequence starts. Place your hands flat under the collarbone, in a straight line. In that position your hands are over the thymus gland right above the heart.

Your goal is to become aware of the texture and quality of the area. Leave your hands long enough to start feeling a sense of ease in the tissues. Does it feel cold or warm? Can you sense any tightness or a sense of blockage as if there is not enough liveliness in the tissues? As you tune into the area you might witness a change in progress.

This work takes place on a subtle level and at times it will challenge your patience but also surprise you with new insights. Remember this is possibly the first time the recipient will experience your touch, so stay only long enough to introduce a first contact.

Slowly move both hands a couple of inches above the middle chest. You are now in contact with your patient's etheric field. Focus on being a clear channel. In your heart burns a flame of *unconditional love*. Always stay in touch with your heart. You are open to any signals, sensory perceptions, changes and shifts in the energy field. Your mental attitude is one of clarity.

After a few minutes, visualize a clear energy field flowing evenly from the recipient's heart center toward his or her head and feet and clearing the recipient's whole field along the way. Stay with the visualization as long as it feels comfortable. By and by, your own intuition will become your guide. Slowly pull your hands evenly away from the area with a gesture of release from the recipient's body.

Your hands move to the top of the head on each side of the crown chakra. The head is very sensitive to touch. It reacts positively to gentle hand contact. For the recipient if the first touch on the chest might have aroused some anxiety, the head touch has a calming effect. Your hands offer comfort, warmth and security. For your hands it is a resting-place, a little oasis. As the recipient soaks in the stabilizing effect of your hands, you make an intuitive assessment of your next move. All the while you are aware of being grounded and centered on your heart vibration.

Sometimes it feels like the recipient needs more stabilizing or maybe your hands need more encouragement so you place your hands over the shoulders. The left shoulder is particularly sensitive to the calming effect of that touch. Having established for both of you a connection that has its own quality, this connection will develop as the session unfolds and will be a guiding force.

The Sequence with the Patient Lying Down

The sequence starts with the chest area. You then move to the throat followed by the head. You will retrace your steps via the throat and the chest. Your next area is the solar plexus and finally the abdomen and the limbs. You may want to turn the person flat on their stomach and do the sequence in the same order on their back, although it is not always necessary.

Chest

Place your hands in an A position around the heart center, your fingers pointed toward the heart and palms directed toward the shoulders. Take time to experience the fullness of the contact. As you stay centered, visualize rays of light starting from the heart center and moving in all directions. Deep within your heart, say a prayer of thanks for the divine energy at work in its sacred aspect of "Love, Light and Life". Stay in tune with the inner reaction of the recipient. Stay in tune with what is communicated to your hands. After a while you may move the palms of your hands slightly out into a straight position over the heart center with hands touching at the fingertips. Stay for a moment and then move your hands into a V position from the heart center, palms touching and fingers down towards the hips. With these three hand positions, you have created a star around the heart center and covered most of the chest area. Stay in tune with the overall feeling that comes from your inner self. At all times make yourself as physically comfortable as possible. (You may need to adjust your position to remain centered). Slowly take your hands away.

Throat

Place your hands in a cradle position, about three inches away around the throat. You are right over the throat center or 5th chakra. You are balancing the Chi or Prana energy when you interlock your fingers, bringing the Yin and Yang to merge and flow. Stay tuned with your "inner", your source of pristine clear energy. (This could be the time to create a mantra, a form of simple affirmation that we may repeat at times, such as "divine love, sacred light, eternal life). Visualize the energy flowing into the fifth chakra or throat center as well as spreading toward the heart and the head center.

Move your hands away.

Head

Place the base of your hands over the ears with fingers stretching toward the chin. Both hands are positioned a couple of inches below the jawbones. Slowly lock your fingers together, shifting your hands position slightly to accommodate the move until your hands are in a cradle position. Check on your breathing, sensing the life energy emanating from your hands. Slowly move your hands away.

The point between eyebrows is the sixth chakra where the pineal gland is located. In that area, you may place your hands directly on the face or experiment a few inches above the face. You may try both ways at different times. Your intuition is always your best guide. With the sixth chakra as center, you will position your hands in a:

1. Straight line over the bridge of the nose with fingers interlocked, so that the palms of your hands cover the temples.

2. Downward in a V line to cover the eyes

3. Upward in an A line toward the hairline.

You have created a star alignment.

Each position is held long enough for you to feel connected wholeheartedly with Chi energy. Repeatedly listen to your heart center as a guide.

Hands-on Healing

Both hands move to the back of the head.

The center point at the back of the head is in tune with the eyebrow center or sixth chakra. With that point as center, you will position your hands to achieve a:

1. "Star" position from the center. The upward line goes toward the top of the head. The downward line toward the base of the skull. The straight line toward the ear lobes.

2. The center point at the base of the cranium corresponds to the pituitary gland, which together with the pineal gland form an important part of the head center. Your fingers are looking for a soft crease at the base of the skull. With that point as center, your hands form an A position with your palms stretching over the back of the ears. This is the place where twelve cranial nerves connect to the spine. It is a strategic area since these nerves connect the surface of the brain to the trunk. You may want to take a pause, while you are tuning to the divine light in your heart where all is love and life. (two to five minutes).

3. Both hands move over the top of the patient's head. Slowly raise your hands right over the crown of the head or 7th chakra. Visualize the divine spark in your heart center merging with the divine spark in the recipient's, flowing down by way of your hands into every nook and cranny within the recipient's body. Visualize each one of the mil-

lions of cells within the organism absorbing divine light. (two to five minutes).

Throat

Fingers interlocking, place your hands one inch or so, above the throat center. Being centered stay quiet for a while and in tune with your own breathing. Visualize a light spreading from the throat center all the way to the feet...then from the throat center to the head, clearing and cleansing along the way (three times)... (two to five minutes)

If you feel like it, this is the time to share with the patient your thoughts about working as a team. She/He may focus about clearing locked up emotions out of the throat's chakra. Ask whether you have permission to release whatever is locked up in the throat such as words never uttered or self-esteem never acknowledged or tears held in.

Slowly slide your fingers away from each other as if you were pulling heavy curtains to let in the light. Visualize unconditional love as light mending the way.

Solar Plexus

The solar plexus is located below the diaphragm in the area where the ribs are no longer attached to the flat bone (sternum). It is the seat of held back emotions and for that matter an area easily destabilized in terms of energy supply. (See chapter 2). You will create a golden star above the solar plexus to restore the recipient's protective energy sheath at the etheric level, in the following manner:

1. Your fingers point in a V position a couple of inches over the solar plexus. As you visualize a golden light starting from that center all the way to the shoulders, slowly slide your hands away from the center in the direction of the shoulders. Release them.

2. Your fingers point in a straight line from the center of the solar plexus. Visualize a golden light stretching from the center all the way to the sides. Slowly slide your hands away as they part from the center and release them.

3. Your hands point in an A position from the center of the solar plexus. Visualize a golden light moving from the center all the way to the shoulders. Slowly move both hands away toward the shoulders. Release your hands.

Abdomen

Move to the right side of the patient, either by standing or sitting. Place your left hand in a standard position below the rib cage over the liver area. The liver acts as a blood filter and is often overstressed and overworked, straining the gallbladder that connects with it. Your fingers are pointing toward the middle of the stomach. Your right fingers form an angle with your left fingers as your right palm is positioned over the upper right abdominal area while the left palm is positioned over the liver.

Take time to adjust to any sensory impressions you may receive. It is also the time to be aware of your breathing, of your grounding. How centered are you? If you feel fatigued or numb, exhale fully through the mouth. This technique will help you to be centered again. If this is a first session, you might discover that the liver area feels cold or blocked up. Give it time. Slowly raise both hands a couple of inches over the area. Leave the right hand still and start pulling slowly with your left hand above the liver, while you visualize the opening of a gate. (2 mn).

In your own words, share a vision of a radiant light flowing through the gate, clearing and healing all cellular tissues in the liver and gallbladder. (You might want to mention a particular color.) Slowly move both hands away and release, asking the receiver to give every cell in the area permission to be in glowing health and light.

Move your position to the left of the patient either by standing or sitting. Place your right hand in a straight alignment below the rib cage, fingers pointing toward the middle of the stomach. Your left fingers make an angle with your right hand. Your left hand covers a diagonal part of the upper abdominal area.

Your right hand covers the area of the stomach, the spleen and the pancreas. This whole area relates directly to the immune system.

The spleen is a ductless gland controlling the activity of the blood's vascular system. Its function is to manufacture white blood cells. Behind stands the left kidney. Next to the spleen, the pancreas is a gland producing the hormone insulin that helps maintain the proper amount of sugar level in the blood. These glands are inhibited by the emotion of grief. Anytime there has been an experience of loss, of sweetness going out of life, a heartbreak, some vital energy gets locked up in that area.

Stay in this position as long as it feels needed. When your hands are ready to move away, you will position yourself for a "pull out" of the spleen area. Your left hand will replace the right in a standard position over the spleen and your right hand gently rests over the heart area. Slowly pull up your *left* hand with great care as if it were attached to a fishing rod. What will come at the end of it, is what needs to be released (blocked up emotions).

Ask the recipient to exhale deeply through the mouth a couple of times while you do the pull out. (Some people suffering from asthma might have a problem with breathing suggestions.) As you slowly pull, ask the recipient whether there is any heartbreak they can remember.... Ask if there is a readiness to let go of the old sense of loss. Ask the patient to clear channels of anything hindering the free flow of love and light with specific others. When the recipient is ready, release the hand away from the body. Gently place your right hand over the area of the "pull out" and ask the recipient to mentally affirm with you "I accept at the cellular level the *joy of being fully alive right now!*".

Place both hands in a V position over the second chakra on the lower abdomen. Ask the patient to breathe in deeply, pushing their belly right out and slowly exhaling through the mouth (three times) and then to resume breathing normally. Leave your hands for a while.

Now your hands are in a double standard position. The right on the stomach area, the left below the navel (5 minutes). Slowly raise your left hand above the lower abdomen until you are about one foot away (2 minutes).

Ask the recipient to let go of whatever is consciously or unconsciously limiting their freedom to be. Let your hand go with the release. Now ask for their full attention, to visualize the inner space within their abdomen filled with light. Encourage each person to view their own color. After a while, have them see their color turn into gold. You may even have them visualize a bouquet of favorite flowers or the seed of a beautiful plant growing in perfect health in their own space.

You are affirming aloud *"This is my own sacred place, it is fully alive and functions in complete health and integrity within my whole system"*.

Place both hands in an A position on the second chakra with palms outstretched toward the groins. Stay long enough to feel centered and in touch with your breathing while aware that you are in the process of closing the session. Both hands separate and in a slow motion above and along the legs, you draw the energy all the way down to the feet. Release your hands.

Closing Affirmation

With the patient still lying down, you stand up facing the feet of the recipient. Gently wrap your hands around both ankles. You are grounding the energy while you stay centered and focused within your own inner silence. Pay attention to your breath gently flowing in and out. (2 minutes)

You need to ground the energy inside each arm, by creating a diamond (fingers pointing up then down) within each fold.

"Deep within me is a divine healing energy. It rests in the feeling of unconditional love, infinite life, and divine light that vibrates throughout my being." (Mental affirmation).

Visualize a golden light flowing out of your eyes and moving from the feet of the recipient to the head and back. (Three times).

Grounding

Have your patient sit down from their lying position and rest for a while. Now you need to ground their energy while they either sit or stand in front of you. Make yourself comfortable as you place both hands around their ankles while their feet are on the ground. (2 minutes)

Now you are both standing up, facing each other. At the same time join your hands in front of your heart chakra. Slowly raise your hands over your crown chakra. In a slow motion, your arms open until they fall down along your sides. Once more your hands join in front of the heart chakra. Slowly take a bow toward each other.

"Thank you for being a healing channel."

Absent Healing

You may send absent healing to anyone, including yourself.

You need to have people's permission. It is key to use their full birth name in healing. If you wish, combine their full birth name and current name.

You may send to a situation, in that case no need for permission.

You Are a Beacon of Light

Your mind acts as a projector directing your thoughts.

1. Make yourself comfortable either standing, sitting or lying.

2. Quieten your thoughts

3. Observe your breathing-quieting down…in and out

4. Focus and visualize as if you had in front of you the person (singular or plural) or the situation you want to send healing to.

5. Wrap them mentally in a halo of divine light coming from your heart and whole self

6. Silently or aloud, as you feel the most comfortable with, express these words

   "I ask my Divine Self to ask the Divine Self within (name the people or the situation you want to heal) to release and recreate what is necessary for his or her highest good. Thank you for being a healing channel."

Hold on to your visualization until you feel ready to let it go

Summary

Hands-on healing is a total experience. The Healing practitioner is tuned to the divine spark in the heart chakra. Whenever we open ourselves to divine guidance, our healing faculties are enhanced. We discover that we are in the light of the One in whom we live and have our being.

CHAPTER FIVE

DANCING WITH LIFE

*"What has been is what will be,
What has been done is what will be done.
God summons each event back in its turn."* (Eccl.1:9)

Early astronomers believed that stars govern destiny. Over many generations they gained understanding of vast cosmic planetary rhythms. They understood that the universe operates in a non linear, recurrent way.

The yearly cycle of seedling, germinating and harvesting evoked religious feelings. Natural observations nurtured belief in the resurrection of life after death. If the life force within a seed is waiting to burst back to life at the right season, could the soul in essence ever die? Not surprisingly, the ancient Egyptians had a blade of wheat as the symbol of everlasting life.

Our evolution is taking place on a planet spinning around its axis. Days, weeks, months, and seasons have a cyclic rhythm. This natural law is an integral part of our lives. Not only is our biological clock affected but all creation becomes a part of the rhythmic motion. The periodicity is reflected in the inhalation and exhalation of our lungs as well as in the beating of our heart. Is there a link between the rhythm of the universe, the development of our consciousness, and the beating of our heart? The Ancient Initiates thought so.

In the "Golden Ass," written by Apuleius in the second half of the second century AD, based on a Greek tale, the hero Lucius praises the Goddess Isis after his initiation into her Mysteries. He sees her as the savior of humanity telling her "The stars move to your orders". The attributes of Isis were those which would be expected from the "Lord of the precession of equinoxes".

What is the Precession of Equinoxes?

The equinox is the specific time of the year when the day is of equal length with the night. It happens twice a year in the spring and the fall.

The phenomenon of precession of equinoxes was discovered in 128 BC by the Greek astronomer Hipparchus of Nicaea. A wobble in the earth's rotation on its axis causes the earth's poles to move very slowly in relation to the solar system. The vernal equinox or the rising sun in the spring, seems to move backward against the celestial sky by thirty degrees every twenty-one hundred years and some. In other words, around every 2100 years, the sun rises in a new constellation of the Zodiac.

Hipparchus's discovery of the precession of equinoxes indicates that before the sun rose in the constellation of Aries on the first day of spring and in the constellation of Libra on the first day of fall, the sun was rising in the constellations of Taurus and Scorpio. Some two thousand years before, the vernal equinox was set in Gemini and the fall equinox in Sagittarius. Since the beginning of the Christian era, the vernal equinox has been in Pisces. Like a cosmic clock ticking approximately every 26,000 years, a complete cycle requires moving through 12 constellations of the zodiac. In this cycle, the earth achieves a complete revolution in the sky against the fixed stars. This is called the "Great Year." The earth's orbit is neither fixed nor circular.

If one reads the sky according to the old wisdom, one sees each age of about 2,100 years, presenting humanity with an opportunity to receive the influence of a particular constellation and to develop new insights, in order to grow in spiritual maturity.

Ancient wisdom tells us that the age of Pisces was an age of devotion nurturing the development of the intellect. In the third millennium and beyond, we are in the age of Aquarius.

The incoming energy that defines Aquarius is the spirit of synthesis or fusion guiding people to move closer together. It is so powerful that only a heart-centered humanity can benefit from it.

The Cosmic Clock Is Ticking

The term "new age" refers to a shift in our spiritual awareness. Inspired by the changing influence in our galactic cycle, our energy or will power needs to charge from our heart, not from our ego or intellect. The ego's role is only to discriminate and make decisions while staying in its own place.

Let's imagine we are a 120-volt wire being adjusted to 240 volts! Don't you think we are in need of a transformer?

Our transformer is our heart. Our power comes from the adjustment of our mind to our new heart energy.

There is no time to waste.

Since we are all related, our own transformation provides the ground for change in others. Let's think for a moment that we are part of a bio-psychic planetary environment and that our circuitry reaches everywhere. The French paleontologist Teilhard de Chardin (1881-1955) antagonized the Jesuit Community to whom he belonged with his unorthodox view of humanity's evolution. To this day his broad view goes far beyond any conceivable scientific model. Teilhard de Chardin saw life as matter becoming more and more complex under the pulse of consciousness. He saw the genetic structure of humanity or anthropo-genesis (anthropo for human, genesis for origin) as an integral part of the science of life[36]. What works within our consciousness is a convergence of three relationships:

- what affects us individually;

- what affects us collectively; and

- what affects us cosmically.

This vision offers guidance and hope. It introduces a new order where manifested life is not mere accident, but the shape matter takes at a certain level of complexity. We are matter at its more complex level! Who's to say that we cannot evolve to a greater level of complexity on a spiral of greater and greater consciousness? This is what Teilhard proposes and calls Cosmogenesis. He sees God as part of our equation. In his vision, spirit is vibrant in the ether where all are joined, influencing each other, supporting each other in the unity of a vast cosmic sphere whose ultimate boundary we cannot imagine!

---

36   La Place de l'Homme dans la Nature. Teilhard de Chardin. Albin Michel Paris 1956.

Are we ready to accept the light energy as it comes to us? It certainly affects our planet. Are we ready to take responsibility as bearers of light? In our global village, where instant electronic communication influences the way we interact and do business, we can marvel at the window of opportunity to re-examine our attitudes about life and each other. The only power of communication worth exploring is the one fueled with heart-centered energy based on the golden rule of cause and effect. What goes out, comes back as all is energy. This understanding leads to a transformation that will change our life circumstances. It demands our participation. Guidance has been offered for so long. It is now time to give back and accept our potential as shining beings. Our goal is to reflect the Heavens as the Heavens reflect us.

The Art of Seeing Anew

Anna Pavlova, the exquisite ballerina who popularized the art of ballet at the beginning of the twentieth century, said once *"somewhere in every one of us, no matter how deep it may be hidden, is a latent germ of beauty. We dance because this germ of beauty demands expression, and the more we give it outlet, the more we encourage our own instinct for graceful forms. It is by the steady elimination of everything which is ugly, thoughts and words no less than tangible objects, and by the substitution of things of true and lasting beauty that the whole process of humanity proceeds." [37]*

---

37   Anna Pavlova, Portrait of a Dancer, p.150. Presented by Margot Fonteyn. Viking Penguin Inc. N.Y.1984.

With every action, with every thought, we write our life story. We have a choice to choose life enhancing thoughts.

Practice

Let's clear each thought of negativity. Let's filter it through our heart. Let's build our boundaries by reflecting on our own opinions, not on other people's. We can firmly decide not to get involved mentally with other people's problems out of guilt or fear but only if we feel there is a positive reason for it. Let's not view their life story out of curiosity or a need to fill a void in our lives. If that happens, we clear our mind right away. When a destructive thought crosses our mind, we focus on its positive alternative and visualize our higher self's ability to flood our heart with healing light. Each time we clear our own mental field, we help others as we clear all the networks we are connected to.

What does not belong to us is a waste of our emotional energy. Let's not give time to tabloids and negative world events. If they happen, let's shift our attention right back to our center filled with light and send a healing to the people or situation Building our boundaries does not mean we do not care about people or events. It means that we are tilling our soil for productive growth and affirming the divine potential in all. By and by, we will sense a difference between a spontaneous movement of the heart to be trusted or an emotional reflex cultivated by social conditioning.

What Affects You Individually

Create your tree of Life.
In the center of your heart visualize a seed born out of love, light and life. (1mn).
The seed falls and settles in the warmth of your abdomen. (1mn).
Observe the seed growing into a tree of light. (1mn).
Its golden leaves reach your head and beyond. (1mn).
Its roots reach your feet and beyond. (1mn).
At the throat level, a nightingale is nesting in its branches. (1mn).
Listen to the song of the nightingale. (1mn).
Can you hear its trill? It is the sound of love mingling with the joy of life. (2mn).
Let the vibration reverberate inside your whole being. (1mn).
Your roots are reaching deep into the nurturing earth. (1mn).
Feel the sap of life moving up along your spine all the way to your brain. (1mn).
In the crown of your head golden leaves dance in the wind of your creativity and your imagination. (1mn).
You are the Tree of your Life!

Create your garden.
For your thoughts to prosper, you need the good soil of your mind. How do you enhance its soil's quality? An open attitude free of prejudice, opinions and unfinished business of the past is a prerequisite to keep the yin and yang quality.
Explore your present attitude. (5mn).

A good soil is enhanced by awareness of the four directions:
Each direction has a meaning to reveal:
North, trust in your destiny.
South, joy of living.
East, inner wisdom.
West, goal of your life.
Meditate on each direction. (1mn each).
Which special meaning has each direction to offer you? (1mn).
Feel the power that each direction inspires in you. (1mn).

Forming your strength.
Create a mental image of the gardener that you are, planting and reaping new thoughts with deep love. (1mn).
Imagine the spirit in nature responding to your caring. (1mn).
Weed out your garden all the time.
It will take all the discipline you can muster, and you will love it!

Prosperity

Prosperity is positive energy flowing into your life. The nature of energy is to circulate everywhere. It is your birthright to build prosperity as long as you do not interfere with somebody else's wellbeing. You may visualize prosperity circulating in any domain of your life such as:

- love relationship;
- friends;
- job;

- health;
- financial ease
- all others.

Creating Prosperity

In your mind's eye, visualize yourself interacting with loving people, with events of a positive nature coming spontaneously into your life. See yourself sharing with others and enjoying freedom and ease of movement. Remember that like attracts like. Choose creative and positive thoughts. Delight in a sensuous experience as you visualize your positive actions and desires on your mental screen. See it in pictures, see it in color. Work out the details. See it happening to YOU and others. It is all right to accept all the good that life has to offer you as long as your good does not harm others. Sort out what is yours from what is theirs, his or hers. Maintain the picture (15 sec.), and let it go into the loving womb of the Universe.

Cosmic Awareness

Could it be that we are instrumental in healing the Cosmos? Let's see in Nature what is new and coming to life. *This way we liberate our imagination from the bondage of finished forms.*

Dynamics of Evolution and Involution

Focus mentally as you visualize with your inner eye the slow process of development from seed to fruit: a seed in focus within your inner eye… changes into a bud …a leaf…a flower… a fruit. (5 mn).

Focus mentally as you visualize the slow process in reverse from fruit back to seed: a fruit… a flower…a leaf…a bud…back to a seed. (5mn).

Formative Forces

On your mental screen visualize a rose. See its delicate beauty, its color. Sense its fragrance. Behold the vision. (5mn).

Behind the vision of a rose stands the idea of a rose. Focus on the quality of beauty, harmony, perfection and joy embodied in its form. (5mn). This is the idea of a rose.

Behind the idea of a rose is its formative force or energy field.

Visualize the energy field of the rose, see it expand. It now vibrates all around the planet. (5mn).

Synchronicity

Your consciousness expands with practice. Your life story unfolds in unison and harmony with others and your environment. The field you live in is no longer linear. It contains its own meaning where events come together as outer manifestations of an interior landscape of potential synchronicity. In the search for a unifying principle between matter and mind, Dr. Carl G. Jung explored the phenomenon of synchronicity which he defined as a meaningful coincidence connected by simultaneity and meaning[38].

All his life, Jung explored the question of a hidden structure or symmetry within the universe unfolding out of nature's pattern and potential chaos. Synchronicity has been defined as the emergence of each novel form implicit or enfolded within the whole system as its potentiality[39]. It has also been seen as a bridge between matter and mind where consciousness arises out of a deeper common ground.

An event of synchronicity is one in which an event coincides with a meaningful pattern of thoughts for a particular individual without a causal principle. It can be seen as a microcosm reflecting the dynamics of the macrocosm as it unfolds simultaneously in the mental and material aspect of a person's life.

---

[38] Psyche and Symbols. C. G. Jung. Anchor Books edition: 1958.
[39] Synchronicity, The Bridge Between Matter and Mind. F. David Peat. Bantam Books, 1987.

One of my favorite examples of synchronicity relates to Dr. Jung's death as told by the writer Laurens Van der Post:

"The afternoon on which Jung died a great thunderstorm raged over his house at Kusnacht, as if nature itself were mobilized to acknowledge the event. Just about the time of his death, lightning struck his favorite tree in the garden where he would sit most every night".

Sacred Time, Sacred Space

You are the measure of all things. The deeper you probe, the more marvelous and meaningful your life becomes. Your awareness and new consciousness, a result of your mental practices, has become second nature and will lead to a life of meaningful coincidences. You live a miraculous life that reflects your inner state of harmonious consciousness. Your space, your time is sacred.

Your human destiny is to have the earth shine like a star. Accept your inner power and release your own light back. You are feeling at home with your healing power

EPILOGUE

No matter what you present, you are divine.
(Ethel Lombardi, *Facts of Life*)

We are in a time of transition. A new reality emerges as the old one decays. At the height of our western, materialistic society, we have to examine our relationship to each other and to the earth in a whole new way.

So powerful a vibration flows out of the Aquarius dispensation that it releases excessive instability from the earth. At the same time, all negative energy of humanity's unfinished business over the last dispensation is coming out. Hope is that our new vision will synthesize the acquired benefits of our previous age, freedom and respect for all sentient beings and the earth, while our ability to channel powerful cosmic energy will heighten as our heart and mind tune to unite their frequencies.

Let's be guided by our new vision.

Cosmic Affirmation

I am centering myself into Myself,

I am centering Myself into my divine space,

I am centering my divine Self in the world,

I am a loving Light in charge of Myself,

I am a loving Light reaching the earth.

To the North, to the East,

To the South and to the West,

I am a loving Light expanding to the Solar System,

I am a loving Light reaching into Galactic Space,

I am Love and Light Dancing with Life.

Epilogue

I Am the Axis Mundi

THIS IS A LIFETIME STUDY.

THERE IS NO GRADUATION DATE!

About the Author

Katia de Peyer. A dancer, movement therapist and healing practitioner, Katia is on the leading edge of the healing movement. Her first book *Dancing with MySelf: Sensuous Exercises for Body, Mind and Spirit* (1991, 2025) introduces her method of inner-centering through movement, hailed by Diane von Furstenberg as a whole new attitude about exercising.

> *Having personally worked with Katia de Peyer for many, many years, I was ecstatic reading her book and I recommend it highly to everyone interested in finding harmony and inner beauty.*
>
> —Diane von Furstenberg

The spiritual path of healing has been Katia's quest for as long as she can remember. Born in France, she studied ballet in Paris and performed at the Théâtre Marigny with the Ballet des Champs-Élysées and at the Moulin Rouge. In Madrid, she studied flamenco and was invited to join the Spanish Company of Maria Rosa in the mid-sixties.

In New York, a successful career as a personal trainer and healer was enhanced by her serious practice of Zen, Yoga, Tai Chi and Sensory Awareness. In 1981 Katia received a ReiKi and MariEl attunement from Ethel Lombardi, the last Reiki master to be initiated in direct line from Mikao Usui, the man who rediscovered Reiki energy in the late 1800's as an ancient key to universal healing.

In Washington DC, Katia created the program "Healing the Body, Mind and Spirit" at the Lombardi Medical Center of Georgetown University. In 1996, Katia made history at G.U.M.C when invited as a healer during surgery. During five hours of total mastectomy and reconstruction, she offered healing to the patient, the operation deemed a great success by the patient and medical team.

Katia was married to the English clarinet virtuoso Gervase de Peyer. She continues her work as a healer and writer, and lives in London and New York.

Wayne Ensrud was born in Minnesota where he received his BFA from the Minneapolis Institute of Art. He met Oskar Kokoschka, the artist-in-residence at the Institute, who profoundly influenced Ensrud's work. Wayne's paintings and drawings are distinguished by their intensity and luminous use of color. His art is life affirming, a celebration of being. Reflecting Katia's vision, Wayne's whimsical drawings evoke the truth and spirit that lie in every form. Further information on this celebrated painter and his work is available at wayne-ensrud.net

Valerie Aubry edited the manuscript. She has been the Law and Social Science Editor at Oxford University Press, New York and a Developmental Editor of textbooks and ancillaries at D.C. Heath in Massachusetts. She is now a freelance editor specializing in memoirs and biographies, self-help books, and social science works and curriculum.

Printed in Great Britain
by Amazon